A
FAR, FAR
BETTER AMERICA

Fred W. Coble

A
FAR, FAR
BETTER AMERICA

Fifth Edition

"A More Perfect Union"
Isn't Coming
It Has Arrived!
(This is it)

Fred W. Coble

Order this book online at www.trafford.com
or email orders@trafford.com

Most Trafford titles are also available at major online book retailers.

Printed in the United States of America.

ISBN: 978-1-4669-8592-6 (sc)
ISBN: 978-1-4669-8593-3 (e)

Trafford rev. 03/13/2013

www.trafford.com

North America & international
toll-free: 1 888 232 4444 (USA & Canada)
phone: 250 383 6864 ◆ fax: 812 355 4082

Dedication

To My Lovely Daughter Claudette.
She Was My Entire Life
Through Her final Years.
My Inspiration, Confidant,
And Advisor.
She's The Reason I Embarked
On
This Awesome Crusade.

PART I

Part I Content

Foreword.. xi
Preface xiii
1.0   Abolish Politics And Unify Our Nation 1
2.0   Eliminate Duplicate Legislatures.................. 9
3.0   Fair and Honest Elections............................ 13
4.0   Reputable Tax Systems............................... 17
5.0   Lawful Jurisprudence 23
6.0   Eliminate Narcotics Trafficking 27
7.0   Homes For Our Homeless 33
8.0   Health Care for All 39
9.0   Fathers For the Fatherless........................... 43
10.0 Modernize Water and Power....................... 49
11.0 Make Education Relevant............................ 53
12.0 Stop Gay Persecution.................................. 67
13.0 Purge Our Harmful Laws............................ 71
14.0 Regain Our Industrial Power 75
15.0 End Our Nation's Poverty........................... 87
16.0 Balanced Lobbying..................................... 91
17.0 Save Our Newborn 93
18.0 Ethnic Blending 101
19.0 Restrain Our Competitive Craze................. 107
20.0 Attack Crime At its Roots...........................113
21.0 Unify our Foundation 119

22.0   Marriages To be avoided 123
23.0   Control Our Maternity Mêlée 133
24.0   Right vs. Left Brain 139
25.0   Level Playing Field 145
26.0   Our Copper Penny Scam 151
27.0   What Are We To Believe 155
28.0   School Violence 159
29.0   And, In Conclusion 163
         Epilogue 165

Foreword

In this version we've identify some twenty of our nation's most egregious flaws.

Which, if resolved, could raise our nation to prominence, solvency, and prosperity never before imagined; gaining, at last, the *More Perfect Union*—once penned, but never allowed.

The objective, of course, is to provide our citizens with the very best our nation can provide.

But life is more than government and economics. Our physical and mental health, can pose overriding concern for our loved one's, our acquaintances, and our society.

Part II has been added to offer insights into several of our perplexing Medical anomalies:

1.0   Muscular Dystrophy
2.0   Multiply Sclerosis
3.0   Overweight
4.0   Heart Failure
5.0   Strokes

6.0 Parkinson
7.0 Alzheimer's
8.0 Apnea
9.0 Acne
10.0 Atrial fibrillation

These medical theories offered are not based on scientific evidence or clinical results, but rather on decades of observations, deductive analysis and a slice of common reasoning.

Comments, agreements, disagreements, etc. are most eagerly welcomed. An online address is available for disagreements, comments, and suggestions:

fcoble@aol.com

Preface

To propose extensive overhaul of our nation's government and social structure might seem irrational, and perhaps half-baked—if the alternative weren't so objectionable.

Our present conditions leave us with much to be desired:

1. Our primary sources of income—our industries—have all been sent to foreign nations.
2. Tens of million workers are out of work, and have little hope of employment.
3. Hundreds of thousands are homeless, and another hundred thousand are living below the poverty level.
4. Duplicate, and extremely expensive legislatures inhabit our federal and state governments.
5. Money subverts our Elections results.
6. Political parties split our nation into warring factions.

7. Our jurisprudence is politicized, and at the mercy of inept juries.
8. Campaign contributors write our laws.
   And the list goes on.

So what can we do about it?

Reinhold Niebuhr helps us contemplate and deal with such concerns:

God grant me the serenity to accept the things I cannot change; <u>courage</u> to change the things I can; and wisdom to know the difference.

There are, of course, many things we cannot change, and we'd be wise to recognize and accept such invincibility; saving our time and concerns for those things for which we can, and should, strive to change.

John Locke explains why suggestions are seldom honored:

New opinions are always suspected, and usually opposed without any reason but because they are not already common.

George Bernard Shaw also offers a bit of wisdom:

You see things as they are; and say, "Why?" But I dream of things that never were; and I say, "Why not?"

Yes! *Believe it or not.* America really *can be* far, far better than it's ever been.

And the reason it is not is open to question.

Oh Yes. *Greed* is arguably a possible reason. But, those with the greed happen to be the very one's who would benefit most from the *Far, Far Better America*. The goose that lays the golden eggs can always be fattened up.

Why our egregious flaws?

Our detrimental conditions can be traced to our Constitution—commonly honored as a *piece de resistance*. We can surmise what the writers had in mind when they wrote our Constitution:

- An Electoral College was included, to undo *unfavorable* election results.
- Election of the president was in the hands of the Congress
- A Bill of Rights was vigorously opposed (See Bill of Rights below)
- A budget-busting compromise created duplicate legislative bodies.
- Swayable and inept jury systems were assured for our courtrooms.
- Investors in the *revolution*[1] were completely refunded, but the fighters were given nothing.

---

[1]   The overthrow is more correctly identified as a coup.

- States may write laws for electing *federal* Congresspersons. (Thus the open primary[1] tactic).

Incidentally, the Constitution did NOT authorize or imply the imposition of political parties.

While we're on our Constitution, it might be fitting to recognize a gross misinterpretation:

Nowhere else in the Constitution—but in the First Amendment—do we read: "Congress shall make no law . . . (????)

It's intriguing as to how this odd wording got into our Constitution.

A large majority, in the original congress, strongly opposed inclusion of a: "Bill of Rights." During ratification, in New York City they continued to viciously fight against the Bill—spreading a flyer with 98 skillfully worded arguments. The opposition failed and a "Bill of Rights" was ratified.

BUT!

The "Losers" drafted the amendment!

Instead of stating that the various rights are protected, it summarily removed Congress from all jurisdictions thereof. There is no *Protection*!

---

[1] Open primaries foster the Raider conspiracy (See Section 3 Honest Elections)

Interestingly, Amend X. states: *"The powers not delegated to the United States [Congress] by the Constitution, nor prohibited by it to the States, are restored to the States respectfully.*

Wallah!

The States (not Congress) are thereby authorized to make laws respecting the establishment of religions, speech, press, assembly, and petitioning of the government.

These implications and advantages of our shrewdly concocted Constitution are being diligently and steadfastly preserved. It's called conservatism.

1.0

Abolish Politics
And Unify Our Nation

Before the ink was dry on our *hallowed Constitution,* our budding nation was split asunder, and has continued to fragment ever since—into hundreds of competing factions.

Jefferson and Hamilton get credit for splitting America into two nasty political camps, and turning our nation into one horrendous Hatfield and McCoy feud. Hamilton insisted that the Federal Government completely rule over all the States, while Jefferson insisted on maintaining State governments.

Friendships are destroyed; enemies created; animosities erupt; and party line voting dominates heated debates in all our legislative body—at the Federal and State levels.

This warfare even inhabits our halls of justice.

We need to ask: what happened to our nation's creed: *to establish a more perfect Union (?)*

The feud was, indeed, an impulsive display of egotism, and was the unspeakable reason that split our nation into hateful political affiliations.

President George Washington pleaded—obviously to no avail—for Congress to remain united and to avoid the same deplorable schism that plagued the British Parliament.

It's possible, in fact probable, that the words: *A more Perfect Union,* were suggest by President Washington.

Sadly, a most shameful consequence of political affiliations is the fact that every President (except George Washington) has been loved and approved by half the nation, while being bitterly despised and rejected by the other half.

Unifying, and strengthening our nation (abolishing political parties) has always been opposed by the parties; that use their organization to control our government.

The number one priority in Congress is the prevention of opposing Presidents from winning re-election.

All attempts—by our President—to improve the nation are scrupulously defeated by the opposing party in Congress.

This behavior is the mandate given Congresspersons by campaign contributors.

Candidates for political offices are hated, not so much for their policies, but for the political party they represent. What sort of *unity* would one call this sort of demeanor?

Our presidents (and congress persons) should be selected, and elected, for their statesmanship and leadership qualities, not for their association with a particular political party.

Plus, they should never come into office carrying the baggage of a political party.

Section 3.0 (*Honest Elections*) explains how we can elect a non-partisan president: *of, by, and for the people.*[1]

While still residing in England—prior to coming to America—our "Founding Fathers" experienced the deplorable behavior in British Parliament, but were not dissuaded from creating the same sort of debacle in our legislative houses of Congress.

Apparently it did concern George Washington, for he spoke impassionedly about such horrific divisiveness.

There's no reason to suffer any further.

Political parties were never suggested or authorized in our constitution, and their elimination would require nothing more than a simple one-sentence Federal law—prohibiting political parties.

Election ballots would simply list the candidates with no reference to political ideologies.

Voters would not be required to register. They would merely show evidence of their citizenship.

---

[1]   An excerpt from President Lincoln's Gettysburg Address.

And our presidents and congresspersons would be choices of the masses—not political party puppets.

Wouldn't it be heart warming watching a *non-partisan Congress* debating legislation?

Instead of being limited to two obstinate, and politically prejudiced-points of view, the debates would be open to an unlimited number of approaches, without reference to parties.

Legislators would be free to vote the *will of the people*—without fear of reprisal from a political party.

Public officials would operate on a level playing held.

Even the courts would take on a new and awe-inspiring image.

Political ideologies would not influence legislature arguments, or verdicts before the courts.

And political efforts to stack the Supreme and district courts would no longer haunt our nation's jurisprudence.

Unity throughout the land

Besides this horrific split—perpetrated by our political parties—there also festers throughout our land a social disease that eats at the very soul of our nation.

Our great nation has always been splintered into hundreds of competing factions, each with their own agendas, objectives, and ideologies.

Hundreds of ethnic, political, religious, racial, and nationality factions recruit members, amass treasuries, and acquire extensive resources and formidable assets. Their objectives, pure and simple, are to gain political influence, and dominance over other factions.

Those that govern our nation (actually, not really our President and Congress) are not about to make efforts to unify our nation, since this would invoke a slippery slope—jeopardizing the status quo.

It's only natural that people with common interests and national nostalgia would gather to enjoy social events and activities.

But when such people aim to use their collective powers to gain social or governmental favors, we have the makings of serious discord, warring feuds, and threatening animosities.

Schools that enroll children from a single international heritage serve to drive thusly enrolled children away from American allegiance, and devotion—as do private, religious, and charter schools, and so on.

Public schools provide far more for our nation's sovereignty and tranquility then mere formal education. They are our greatest means for establishing national unity.

Public schools prepare our children to deal with our complex society—familiarizing them with all nationalities, ethnicities, intellects, and sexes.

As for allegiances to foreign nations, **all** *immigrants*, upon application for American citizenship—must swear:

I hereby declare, on oath, that I absolutely and entirely renounce and abjure all allegiance and fidelity to any foreign prince, potentate, state, or sovereignty, to whom or which I have heretofore been a subject or citizen; that I will support and defend the Constitution and laws of the United States of America against all enemies, foreign and domestic; that I will bear true faith and allegiance to the same,—and so forth.

Those of us, who are citizens by virtue of our birth or other such means, are, in deed, bound by the very same oath.

Waving an American flag, reciting the pledge of Allegiance, and singing the National Anthem does not fulfill our citizenship commitment.

To be an *American* one must renounce ideologies and allegiance to all foreign sovereignties, and assume the pride of an American citizen, through and through.

Imagine the power and influence our nation would enjoy if all splintered factions were to join in one great concerted effort to unify our objectives and efforts, eliminating organizational titles and operating under the same charter.

In the early 1940's we approached such a unity when our entire nation joined in one common cause—to win WWII.

When non-American groups band together to preserve *their* social rights, or allegiance to their fatherlands, other factions and people intuitively sense a threat to their respective liberties, influence and freedoms.

In a true sense this banding together is tantamount to the old expression: "putting a chip on one's shoulder."

2.0

Eliminate
Duplicate Legislatures

Almost nothing in government is more wasteful and costly then duplicating our organizations. And our duplicated legislative bodies—at the federal and State levels—are horrendous, outrageous, and extremely expensive.

Almost impossible to believe is the fact that such a travesty was ever contrived, and that it continues to exist.

Well! It all started behind closed doors in Philadelphia, circa 1787. The framers of our Constitution were arguing over the number of elected representatives each state could send to Congress.

The larger states wanted representation proportional to the number of people being represented. The smaller states—fearing the larger states would dominate the debates—wanted equal representation from every state.

Thus: *the Great Compromise*—certainly nothing for which a great nation need be proud.

Even if this disgusting duplication had a modicum of rationale at the federal level, it certainly wouldn't justify duplicate legislations in every one of our States.

The House of Representatives is not only one horrendous drain on the economy, costing in excess of billions of dollars each year, but is also a fifth leg on the proverbial stool—being one horrific logjam in the legislative process.

Our Senates—Federal and State's—are fully capable of representing the needs of the nation and enacting all the legislation needed to run efficient governments.

Disgraceful too, is the disgusting and offensive *jury maunderings* taking place in every state—mapping out electoral districts—invariably carved out to benefit the party in power.

The Houses of Representative, at both the federal and state levels, should be *eliminated*. This could be accomplished with little ripple in the legislative process.

Of course, an amendment to the Constitution would be required, and a number of Representatives would be transferred into the appropriate Senates.

Our Senate's mission and scope should also be re-evaluated. Basically, the Federal Senate should be a clearinghouse for settling problems arising between states.

It should *not* be in the business of generating problems or pacifying the special interest groups.

Two and a half centuries have been more than enough time to formulate adequate sets of laws. The number one mission should be: the purging of tens of thousands of laws that are no longer applicable, necessary, or enforceable.

Then the remaining laws should be revised to clarify, simplify, and remove ponderous legalese. When the proposals in Section 4.0 (*Reputable Tax Systems*) are enacted, nearly every tax law would be eliminated.

Sub-committee gamesmanship

Subcommittees are excellent means for providing Congress with the pertinent intelligence needed for formulating meaningful, equitable, and needed legislation.

They should never, however, be used as a forum for engaging in political rancor, such as the airing of our President's personal life.

The hideous practice of grabbing control of subcommittees, and controlling procedural rules, by the majority party should be a practice of the past.

Legislators should be free to voice the *will of the people*—a custom for which they've never been free to do. Legislative debates should never be limited to polarized motivations.

So, when the day comes when we have a president *of and for the people*—a truly great leader—and when the plague of politics is forever erased from our nation, our governmental bodies may finally be organized into efficient, economical, streamlined, and well-oiled legislative machines.

3.0

Fair and Honest Elections

In a true Republic, representatives—chosen by the people—consider the people's wishes, needs, and desires in all matters, and are charged with the responsibility of representing those needs and wishes in our legislative bodies. This is *not* what's been taking place over the centuries.

Our elections are for Fustians[1]—with candidates selling their souls to the highest bidder. We're stacking our legislative chambers with the likes of Judas Iscariots—ready and willing to betray their constituents to campaign contributors—for a million pieces of silver.

Until ALL financial and gift contributions to election campaigns are declared illegal, we will *never* have a true Republic.

---

[1]   Relating to a medieval character who sold his soul to the devil for power and knowledge.

If our government were to pay all campaign expenses it would cost each citizen only several dollars for each campaign.

Our great nation is deserving of honest and highly qualified Presidents and Congresspersons—not political lackeys.

Of course, if our election campaigns were fully financed and managed by our government, any Tom, Dick, or Harry would want to run for public office.

We would need a method for narrowing our candidate's lists to those best qualified and capable of serving—not popular celebrities, actors or fast-talking pitchmen.

Selecting candidates could be accomplished much like our process for certifying professionals, such as: doctors, lawyers, architects, and CPAs. These professionals are required to *compete* via written and oral tests, to prove their qualifications.

Applicants for public offices should be required to do no less. They should compete via written and oral tests, submit to FBI security checks, and provide complete and authenticated résumés.

The government would then use video recordings (CDs and DVDs), mail, newspapers, radio broadcasts, and television debates to acquaint the public with their qualifications, attributes, and experiences.

There would be no need for primary elections, presidential conventions, or an Electoral College. The vice president (a potential president) should be the first runner-up in the presidential election, giving the choice to the people, not some political party, or president.

With public officials obligated exclusively to the people, our governing bodies would certainly take on a new and remarkable character.

We would finally have a bona fide Republic—*that this nation, under God, shall have a new birth of freedom—and that government of the people, by the people, for the people, shall not perish from the earth.*[1]

By eliminating the Houses of Representatives, political parties, and election campaign skullduggery, our elections would narrow to non-partisan goals.

A national mandate for these reforms, proposed herein, would catapult our nation to heights greater than ever imagined.

This undoubtedly sounds like a wild-pipe-dream, much like President Kennedy's dream of sending our men to the moon.

---

[1]   Excerpt from Lincoln's Gettysburg address

4.0

Reputable Tax Systems

A safe, secure, and tranquil society requires a well established, organized, and regulated government. This obviously, calls for considerable amounts of money. It's only right and just that we pay for all these services and our wellbeing—in proportion to our derived benefits.

Those who derive little from our nation's resources, of course, should be expected to pay proportionately smaller tax rates.

Our income tax system should never be used for any purpose other than collecting income taxes—based solely on a person's periodic income[1].

Numbers of dependents, age, marital status, IRA contributions, educational expenditures, disabilities, and the like, should never be considered in the tax calculations.

---

[1]   Income to be defined by a Government publication

Received Social Security payments should never be considered income, and should never be considered relevant to income tax matters.

Computing one's income taxes should not require the services of accountants or tax experts.

A proposed tax plan

Our total incomes, for a set periods of time, should be multiplied times a single percentage—with absolutely *no deductions* or *adjustments* factored in. Definitions of *incomes* should be published and made readily available to every citizen—via mailings, newspapers, web sites, and other means.

Deductions are not only counter-productive, but are a source of irritation, confusion, misdirection, fraud, and abuse, and an excuse for publishing hundreds of obscene forms and instructions.

Forms and instructions should not be a part of the income tax calculations. Hundreds of forms merely complicate and confuse what could, and should be a simple calculation of one's tax obligations.

People who require special dispensations, such as: the elderly, disabled, or those with children, should be properly compensated, but **not** via our *income tax system.*

We could: downsize the IRS staff (at Federal and State levels); eliminate millions of tons of documentation; and re-coup billions of tax dollars presently lost through waste, fraud, and abuse.

State Taxes

One horrific income tax problem plaguing states is the movement of citizens between states and the claiming of addresses in bordering states, plus the confusion of living in one state and receiving salaries from another.

All State income taxes **should be eliminated**. The Federal Government—after collecting taxes from all the nation's citizens would forward payments to the states, commensurate with the taxes collected from the citizens of each state—plus any *special needs*.

Since consumer purchases are proportional to incomes, sales taxes could also be factored into the federal income tax rate and included in the remittances to the states.

Gas taxes could also be factored in, thereby eliminating the state's tax collecting functions.

All these policies would not only save hundreds of billions in operating costs, but would also result in net revenue increases.

To keep the entire tax preparation simple, as the plan goes into effect, the sum of all incomes could be multiplied times 20%.

This would allow everyone to drop the last figure of their total income, and simply multiply the result times two. Keep in mind that this replaces all state income taxes, and sales taxes.

Although 20% may appear like a drastic reduction for those in the highest income brackets (for many decades in the 70% levels) we should bear in mind that many in the high income brackets pay little or no income taxes—as a result of *creative account practices.*

Taxes, from those with incomes in the millions, would actually increase substantially. Such people might even welcome the chance to play an honest role in the nation's strength and vitality—as opposed to feelings of guilt and being left out. And of course, losses from waste fraud and abuse would also be drastically reduced.

With the elimination of all deductions and clear visibility (by the IRS) of all incomes, the net revenues should be far larger than present receipts.

After the initial trial period, the multiplier percentages could be adjusted to insure adequate revenue to support the federal government and the states.

To mitigate the federal *Cash Flow Needs*, federal taxes could be paid quarterly, tertiary, or semi annually—eliminating the need for employee *tax withholding.*

Should any of the states experience significant shortfall, they could supply their Federal Senators with records, and apply for adjustments.

With retail outlets no longer required to calculate and report sales taxes, their bookkeeping tasks and related expenses would be greatly reduced. Businesses would also benefit from the elimination of employee tax withholding, and Social Security collections.

The 20 percent figure is suggested for simplicity and to illustrate the general idea of our proposed income tax remedy. When these proposals make it through Congress, and become law, the wording will probably sound somewhat different. Of course, these enormous cost savings will admittedly cause huge job downsizings. IRS and State tax collectors could be retained for some period of time while tax laws are being revised and eliminated.

5.0

Lawful Jurisprudence

In recent years, our news media has exposed one of our nation's most egregious flaws: the manner in which lawyers and juries can rape our nation's jurisprudence.

To understand why this happens, over and over again, we need to appreciate how and why our jury system came into being.

Long before our *American Revolution,* the model of our present jury system was already in use in England. While still living in England, the framers of our Constitution had much experience with England's jury system.

They loved it. They knew only too well how skilled (and expensive) barristers were able to finagle juries—of limited knowledge and legal experience.

This invariably tips the scales of justice in favor of the wealthy, while those who can't afford expensive attorneys are at the mercy of providence.

So it comes as no surprise when innocent verdicts are rendered in trials where evidence is overwhelmingly to the contrary.

Our framers apparently didn't want *trials by jury* to be overlooked. Three times, in our Constitution, they mention the right to *trial by a jury*: Article III, Section 2, of the original Constitution, states, in part: *The Trial of all Crimes, except in Cases of Impeachment, shall be by jury;* Amendment VI states: *In all criminal prosecutions, the accused shall enjoy the right to a speedy and public trial, by an impartial jury* (impartial, isn't that a hoot?).

Finally, Amendment VII states: *In Suits at common law, where the value in controversy shall exceed twenty dollars, the right of trial by jury shall be preserved.*

Jury selection is a laborious, time consuming, and very costly process, fostering incompetence, prejudice, and false testimonies.

While serving as foreman on four juries I was appalled by the false responses to questions given by prospective jurors—to get on the jury.

It also became eminently clear that many of the jurors remained ignorant or indifferent to the evidence.

Jurists were often recalcitrant in their refusal to accept definitions of certain legal terms, such as pre-meditation.

Our appellate and district courts have no juries. Attorneys can't pull the shenanigans being perpetrated on lower-court juries.

And verdicts are adjudicated with a thorough understanding of the laws.

Replacing juries with panels of judges would instill credibility in our court system, and would streamline our entire jurisprudence—cutting costs and lightening the court calendars.

Of course, Amendments to our Constitution would be required. But gaining a truly reputable jurisprudence, and the elimination of the shameful and misguided jury system, would be well worth the time and effort.

Matlock and Perry Mason are wonderful on the TV screens, but their imitators are deplorable and revolting in the courtrooms.

Lifetime appointment of judges

And while we're solving the gross miscarriages of justice we would be woefully negligent if we failed to question lifetime appointments of judges to the bench.

Granting human beings the preeminence of supernatural powers is indefensible.

That political Presidents can actually hand pick USA Supreme Court justices (who happen to share the same political ideology) is almost more than one can possibly stomach.

These *supernatural beings* just happen to have the final word on decisions concerning constitutional compliance.

The fact that most cases are handed down with the court split along political party lines is outrageous and indefensible.

After genuine adjudication and research there shouldn't be different interpretations of the Constitution.

First and foremost, no judge should ever be given lifetime appointments. Secondly, no judge should ever be *appointed* by anyone. They should be *elected* to reasonable terms and subject to replacement at election times. A wise and just judge could conceivably be reelected in perpetuity. Their terms should be longer than for other public officials, and they shouldn't have term limits.

The Senate (our new non-partisan Senate) should review all candidates for district and federal court appointments and provide a list of recommended nominees. The names of district and Supreme Court judges could be listed on the presidential ballots with a choice for-or-against nominated candidates.

Since voters would have little or no knowledge of a candidate's qualifications and experiences, they (the voters) could rely on our (non-partisan) Senators' recommendations, and various news media reports. But above all, Judges should never be insulated from public indignation when their performance proves to be biased, prejudicial, resentful, or abhorrent.

6.0

Eliminate Narcotics Trafficking

Yes! We can have zero narcotics trafficking. The proclaimed: "Drug War" be damned. The solution is quite simple and virtually without cost.

We know that narcotic trafficking is one of our nation's most profitable enterprises—perhaps a backbone to our economy—and that money alone is the sole motivator.

Since children are the easiest targets for narcotics addiction, easily influenced students are offered attractive sums of money to get fellow students hooked on narcotics.

If there were no money to be made, narcotic sales on the playgrounds would amount to zilch. In fact, if there were no profit in the manufacture and sale of narcotics there would be no trafficking.

The solution

With a simple stroke of the President's pen, all trafficking could be brought to a screeching halt. The government should take complete control of the production, distribution, and sale of all narcotics. To accomplish this, the government would merely issue contracts to companies capable of producing the narcotics.

These narcotics would be delivered to pharmacies throughout the nation where addicts could buy them at or below cost—far below the costs offered on the street.

Note: This should never be construed as "Legalized Narcotics." For *legalizing* narcotics would allow anyone to produce, advertise, and distribute narcotics—a sure way to addict the masses.

The key results of this solution should be rather obvious. With all the money eliminated, tons of illegally produced narcotics wouldn't be worth the plastic in which they're wrapped.

Addicts could *come out* in the open, apply for rehabilitation, and buy pharmaceutically packaged narcotics at a small fraction of the street cost.

Each package would include guidance, warnings, and information about clinics and medications to assist in breaking the addiction.

The names of the buyers and their purchases would not be released.

Addicts could obtain a card from a doctor certifying that they are addicts. This would allow them to make the necessary purchases.

Non-addicts should be able to buy small quantities of certain narcotics by providing identification and by signing a statement citing their intended use. This *questionable* effort would be necessary to completely eliminate street traffickers.

With the government taking over the production and distribution of narcotics, most narcotics users serving time in prison could be released and put on probation—nearly emptying most prisons.

Many would argue that this program would encourage many children (and grownups) to take advantage of the availability of narcotics, increasing the number of addicts at a faster rate.

The big attraction for narcotics—as with alcohol and cigarettes—however, is NOT availability.

Experimentation would be discouraged in absence of peer pressure, along with strong guidance from parents and teachers.

Printing the skull and crossbones on each package and including explicit warnings would also help discourage would-be experimenters.

As with any high-minded and far-reaching remedy—aimed at solving earth-shaking catastrophes—there emerge numerous antagonists. Foremost will be those presently benefiting, directly or indirectly, from ungodly windfalls from the narcotics war. Such benefactors number in the millions, and are spread across the economic spectrum.

Of course, I've no idea how these benefactors might be persuaded to surrender such a luxury. My hope is that they've already amassed such a lucrative fortune that their need to acquire more might not be all that necessary. Perhaps they might use their fortunes to make even more—on the Stock Market, etc.

Some might reason that legalizing alcoholic beverages, by repealing prohibition, succeeded in squelching organized crime. And, so it did. Legalizing the production and distribution of alcoholic beverages took the profit motive from the hands of organized crime and turned it over to highly advertising mass markets.

And we can see all around us the tragic results of legalizing alcoholic beverages. Organizations such as MADD—dealing with tens of thousands of deaths on the highways—are keenly aware of the deplorable tragedies.

Whereas, *nationalizing* narcotics would curb and control the distribution of narcotics to those addicted.

Hopefully, amide those benefiting from the humongous narcotics wind falls, there might be a number of conscientiously minded citizens that would put the good of our nation and the survival of our children above their ill-gotten gains.

This plan would prevent tens of thousands, perhaps millions, of children from becoming narcotics addicts, and criminals of every type and severity.

Police departments are losing the Drug War and, by all indications, show there is no perceived hope. All efforts have failed miserably and the future holds no hope of ever winning.

Accepting the *status quo* is turning our backs on the many millions of addicts, as well as those of future generations.

Parents of addicted children know all too well how devastating is the horrible curse.

Repeating: A simple law establishing our government as the sole producer, distributor, and retailer of all narcotics would immediately and forever eliminate all narcotics trafficking—and much of the resultant crimes.

7.0

Homes For
Our Homeless

Out of sight is out of mind, particularly when this concerns our hundreds of thousands of homeless men, women, and children, hidden away in our worst sections of towns, and never seen in restaurants or shopping centers.

Sadly absent from our TV documentaries are scenes depicting the horrible conditions under which our homeless people are living (barely surviving)—scenes that would bring this crisis to the public's attention.

Truth be known, our apathetic and heartless public probably doesn't want to know about the lives and living conditions of our homeless people.

In attempting to solve this problem we should first know from whence these men, women, and children are coming.

Not geographically or demographically. But rather: mentally, physically, and emotionally.

References to this subject are usually misleading and often cloaked in sick humor.

Anyone with a modicum of awareness, decency, and compassion is aware of the myriad causes that bring these ill-fated people to where they are today.

Mentally challenged, hopelessly addicted, physically inept, and asylum deportees, are at a loss when attempting to find and hold any sort of employment.

California governor, Ronald Reagan, intent on showing a balanced state budget, turned the mentally challenged into the streets.

The public occasionally gets a glimpse of the results of this inhumane act when a fatal stabbing hits the headlines. Otherwise the public is spared the horror.

Token meals several times a year and occasional army cots or pads on the floor of an armory when the weather drops below freezing may salve the conscience of some of us, but we know we can, and should, do far more.

These *human beings*—living in the richest nation in the world—certainly shouldn't be living in squalor, disrespect, and hunger.

Some citizens with adequate life styles hoping to allay a twinge of guilt may be inclined to pose the question:

Are we our brother's keeper?

I would leave that question for each of us to answer.

When the *Great Rabbi* told his disciples they must love their neighbor as themselves, a disciple asked: *And who is my neighbor?*

The Master Rabbi told the parable of the Good Samaritan.

For those unfamiliar with the parable: T*he Good Samaritan (*an outcast of the Jewish community) *found a severely injured man lying along the highway—who had been passed-over by several holy people. He bent down, nursed the man's wounds, carried him into town, and told an innkeeper that he (*the Samaritan*) would pay all the man's bills the next time he came by*[1].

Homeless Remedy

I do believe there is a phenomenal remedy: Now that the *cold war* is over and we have no formidable enemies in the world, we are closing many of our military bases throughout the country.

These bases are literally small cities, capable of supporting large populations of homeless personnel.

We could proceed with the dismantling of all weaponry—leaving intact the living quarters, food and dining facilities, transportation capabilities, clothing storerooms, housing and medical facilities.

---

[1]   New Testament: Luke, 10:30-37

Homeless people could occupy the living quarters, be fed in the base dining halls, and receive clothing from the storerooms.

These newly housed people could assist, as they are mentality and physically able, in the upkeep, maintenance and running of the base operations. Physicians and psychologists could be made available as necessary.

A core of military personnel could remain for an interim period to perform duties in the dining hall, laundry room, motor pool, guard shack, and so on.

The primary objective of this concept is to make facilities and conditions available that would encourage self-pride, purposeful living, and a sense of dignity. Admittedly, there would be attitude and behavioral problems, but these people are human, and as American citizens, deserve our compassion and care.

We cannot leave this subject without looking in on the lives and conditions in which these people live. Mel Brooks produced a profound motion picture: *Life Stinks*, which took us inside the lives and conditions of many of the homeless.

One couldn't escape the reality of the conditions homeless people have to endure.

Trash is their only possession, dumpsters their source of nourishment.

Cardboard boxes and crates provide their shelter, and secluded alleyways their bathrooms.

People who've never attempted to communicate with these homeless, dare to blame them (the homeless) for their circumstances. One need only spend a few minutes with several homeless people to realize they haven't the mental aptitude or perseverance necessary for performing even the most menial of tasks.

Genetics have robbed these folks of the wherewithal we take for granted. To experience a most exuberant emotion, hand a homeless person a ten-dollar bill. Be prepared for the most heart wrenching exhilaration you'll ever experienced.

Suggesting we citizens should care enough about the homeless and downtrodden to insist our government takes steps to house, clothe, and feed the homeless, smacks of socialism, liberalism, and any number of caustic slanders.

Most of us will sleep peacefully at night, and hopefully be spared visits from the *Spirit-of-Christmas-Future*.[1]

---

[1]   From the Christmas Story by Charles Dickens

8.0

Health Care for All

It costs more to administer our nation's health care than to pay for all the services of providers. All indirect costs (over 200 billion) are borne by the taxpayer. We can eliminate most administrative costs—*without destroying our healthcare-provider industry*—by implementing a rather simple plan, as follows:

Divide the USA into six health-care districts—corresponding to the six time zones.

Have insurance companies compete for service contracts for managing the health-care districts.

Providers (Doctors, hospitals, Specialists, etc.) would collect a co-pay and record the identification, and medical procedures for each patient served.

The sum records of services provided would be itemized, and mailed or faxed to the appropriate district-insurance companies.

The insurance companies would pay their zone providers and bill the federal government.

The Federal Treasury would send monthly (or bi-weekly) checks to each of the six health-care district managers.

Congress, in concert with the AMA and other medical associations, would compile and price out a standard health-care price list for medical procedures.

Doctors would have the option of receiving payments from this standard health-care price list, or of billing their patients, as usual.

Patients would have the choice of a pay-for-services provider or a standard health care billing provider.

Prescription drugs would cost a co-pay of several dollars.

This plan could eliminate the following:

- Medicare & Medicaid
- All private health care plans
- All HMOs
- All company health-care plans
- Dozens of federal bureaus
- Millions of tons forms and records
- Billions in administrative costs

A most valuable by-product would be the virtual elimination of waste, fraud, and abuse.

Health-care zone managers (insurance companies) would constantly review the providers' charges for legitimacy and accuracy.

By this, we mean insurance companies, having won a contract with a specified price plus fixed fee, would gain or lose depending on how closely each of the provider's costs are met.

We're talking here about hundreds of billions of dollars eliminated from our nation's healthcare costs. Far more than the nation's total provider charges.

This would *shift* the money from indirect costs into gainful use.

Administrative costs contribute absolutely nothing toward healing and should be classified as unnecessary waste.

Providers would be relieved of the voluminous paperwork, and the federal government would drop thousands of paper shufflers from their payrolls.

Health care would become a simple matter of providing services where and when needed.

From the billions of dollars saved, the federal government could help finance construction of hospital facilities in isolated towns throughout the nation, and subsidize physicians in remote locations.

Heath care for everyone should rank as the nation's highest order of importance. The homeless would most definitely be included.

Just a note concerning the condemnation of: *Socialized Medicine, Universal Health Care, or the* any of the other confrontational names being thrown about.

This six-territory management plan does not (repeat, does not) take private industry out of the process.

In fact, the simplicity of the insurance company's profit and loss statements would significantly improve their profit margins.

9.0

Fathers
For the Fatherless

Scientific studies highlight troubles affecting children raised exclusively by mothers. We needn't iterate or dwell on the countless ways children are impacted.

Tens of millions of fatherless children live in foster homes, orphanages, and with single working mothers, and the number is constantly rising. Basic math gives us a good idea of the root causes of this sad dilemma. About thirty million women are looking for husbands—most with children desperately needing fathers.

Unfortunately, there are less than a million marriageable men available. Exacerbating this crisis is the ever-shrinking number of heterosexual men. (See Section 12: Stop Gay persecution).

This shrinking phenomenon stems from the fact that the great majority children are born of bisexual parents.

As we explain in Section 12, approximately 60% of our society is bisexual, and most of them don't know they are bisexual.

Bisexuals are naturally drawn toward what is accepted as the "norm" and they are intent on generating nuclear families.

Their offspring are almost entirely bisexual and homosexual.

Genetically, the chances are rare that a heterosexual child will be in the bunch.

Most of our 50% divorce rate can be attributed to bisexuals who lack the inner resolve needed to persevere life-long relationships.

The results: an ever-increasing number of divorces and single parents, left to seek out the mysteries of life—with their children becoming the real tragedy.

These children have two strikes against them:

1) They are somewhere between bisexual and homosexual, and
2) They have no male image to emulate.

Note: Homosexual fathers cannot alter children's sexual orientation (it is completely gene controlled) but could at least provide a male image—as espoused by our society at large.

Solution:

There is a remarkable—but obviously contentious—solution.

Well-established families could adopt one or more of the single-parent families.

Note: California is considering a proposal to authorize multiple parents.

Polygamy? Yes! To many—brainwashed and vulnerable non-thinkers—this is a dirty word; frowned upon by many religious groups.

Polygamy was widely accepted (never condemned) in the Old Testament of our Judea/Christian Bible. And, there are no specific condemnations of polygamy in the New Testament.

Some may argue that Paul, a disciple of Jesus, advocated "one wife." Actually he was stating that for a man to be a deacon in the synagogues he should have *a* wife (possibly to eliminate homosexual deacons).

He didn't say "only one wife" and he never said that non-deacons should be limited to one wife.

In the Gospels, Jesus, the founder and author of the Christian faith, never put a limit on the number of wives.

The Islamic religion allows a man four wives. Many societies around the world place no limit on the number of wives.

Only the American legal system bans the practice.

Regardless of how we may feel or believe about polygamy, the fact remains that our children from single parent homes deserve a far, far better life.

If the tens of millions of fatherless children are to be nurtured and reared by loving fathers, these fathers will likely have their own families.

As in other societies, the first wives would have to approve any additional wives and any of their offspring.

Many sharing wives might be pleasantly surprised when they discover the limitless advantages of sharing their homes (and many of the chores) with a second homemaker.

Years ago the following article entitled *Women need wife support*: appeared in the New York Times paper:

Now that women have solidly earned their place in the work force, many find themselves still yearning for something men often have: wives.

Workingwomen (married and un-married) are discovering what many women have known since time and immemorial: marvelous things can happen when "wives" are added to the household.

Brigham Young required men to adopt as many women as they could house and feed.

Women who couldn't be provided for were left along the trail to die.

Our society's dirty-minded men (most of who probably indulge in extramarital affairs) characterize Mormons as sex perverts. Truth be told, polygamous men are unlikely to indulge in extra-marital affairs.

Even though multiple marriages hurt no one, nor influence adversely the integrity of conventional families, hoards of judgmental people feel compelled to bring down the full force of the law.

Anti-polygamy laws have no moral, spiritual, legal, cultural, or social justification. They are nothing more than selfish demands of insecure and possessive people.

Perhaps the anti-polygamists might switch their condemnations to the millions of couples living together without a marriage certificate.

The time is long past for *we-the-people* to come to our senses and cast aside outrageous dogma. Many vintage minds have clear visions that could re-shape our horizon, and it's time we embark on the true essence of life and its meaning.

Life is far too short, and far too precious to squander on misshapen prejudice, and warped bias. Our nation's children with single parents suffer every moment we refuse to open our minds and our hearts.

10.0

Modernize
Water and Power

Prior to WWII rubber was considered a highly valuable and indispensable product. Our nation, it seemed, would be forever dependent on rubber for its industrial survival.

Then along came a product called neoprene. That did away with our reliance on rubber.

In like manner, we are nearing the crossroads where oil producers will no longer hold our nation hostage.

Many lubrication applications that previously required oil have already been replaced with synthetics. Of course, oil will continue to be used as the source for hundreds of by-products.

Not only is our dependency on gasoline, for our cars, power plants, and sailing vessels a danger to our health, but is likewise a threat to our homeland security—because of the Middle East crisis.

We must free ourselves from oil producing nations and giant oil companies.

One alternate technology, perfected decades ago, is able to produce electricity and pure water without the use of moving parts, petroleum, or external power.

This technology—which has supplied electricity and water for **all** our manned space travel—has been proven safe and reliable.

They call this technology "Fuel Cells." Fuel cells combine an oxidizer such as oxygen and a gaseous fuel such as hydrogen to produce electricity and water.

Fuel cells, installed in automobiles, could generate the electricity needed to power electric motors for propelling automobiles—without the use of gasoline or combustion engines.

They could also be used in homes to provide all the needed electricity and water, and likewise in seagoing vessels.

Antagonists argue against the development of fuel cells claiming difficulties and high cost of producing hydrogen. Bear in mind that Germany—using 17th century technology—produced billions of cubic feet of hydrogen—to fill their giant dirigibles.

Hydrogen happens to be in great abundance in the atmosphere, and in water. Water is H^2O.

The time has long come to break the bonds of our oil entrapment.

We need to disprove claims that hydrogen is difficult to produce. We sat out to land a man on the moon and now we must set out to produce hydrogen cheaply and in great quantities.

In time, a simple device will extract oxygen and hydrogen from the atmosphere and feed them directly into fuel cells.

And, as everyone in the manufacturing business knows: as production quantities increase, the cost per item drops commensurately.

The quantities of fuel cells produced could easily exceed that of automobile production. Try to imagine fuel cells in homes, cars, water vessels, business facilities, recreational vehicles, motor homes, medical facilities, recreational parks and more.

We're talking many billions of fuel cells. The costs would eventually be less than that of our home television sets. And our nation would be freed from the enslavement to oil.

11.0

Make Education Relevant

Education has long been peddled as a magic elixir for our nation's security, economy, employment, and general welfare—a glorious panacea to solve all our nation's problems.

This assertion is made in spite of the fact that men with virtually no formal education were the very ones responsible for elevating our nation to the greatest industrial power in the world; names like: Edison, Howe, McCormick, Fulton, Bessemer, Ford, Wright Brothers, Faraday, Marconi, De Forest, Goodyear, Watts, and Fitch.

What's so relevant about these great achievements is that these men accomplished great feats without the aid of formal education.

Milton S. Hershey, my *foster father*, with a third grade education built the largest chocolate corporation in the world, and an entire town for over 5,000 people.

For disadvantaged children, Mr. Hershey built the nation's most luxurious home/school—presently worth over 6 billion dollars.

In a Hotel-Hostess Room, at a Military Logistics Conference, a Chief Executive Officer of one of the nations largest electronic firms confided: *We can hire all the brightest engineers we want, but are unable to find creative geniuses who can come up with original ideas and significantly advance the art of electronics technology.*

Two personal experiences:

Over decades and expenditures of trillions of dollars the USAF built a nationwide radar defense system with hundreds of fighter interceptors jets—standing on alert 24/7. The mission was to defend our nation against possible attacks by USSR bombers.

Mock exercises to test our vulnerability were periodically conducted, and results usually revealed that a large majority of USSR bombers could hit vital targets unabated.

1) Working with an Air Force Colonel I designed an Intercept Computer (CP-33D) (See Fig.1.) for the Defense Department.

It enabled our Radar controllers to direct aircraft intercepts. Five Air Force generals witnessed three

F-86 jet aircraft intercepting an Air Force jet. All three interceptors scored perfect hits.

The two Star General ordered construction of 25 of the computers.

Fig 1. CP-33dD Computer

2). During our General's briefings, a Colonel complained that his Air-to-Ground radio transmissions were not being received.

I described a console I had built for this purpose. The General directed me to build such units for each of his 16 radar sites. (See Figure 2)

Fig. 2. Air to ground Communications console

The consoles were able to discern radio signals considerably lower in amplitude than the ambient noise levels.

I mention these two examples as illustrations of the type of solutions that innovative thinkers can derive—without advance academic achievements.

Such Thinkers are genetically right-brain dominant. (See chapter 24. Right & Left Brain Influences).

Innate Intelligence

Our schools provide excellent opportunities for intellectual students to excel and reap bountiful rewards.

Below-average students, on the other hand, have difficulty comprehending and memorizing data from volumes of textbooks—written primarily by and for intellects.

Employers tend to hire on the basis of high school grades and diplomas, although more than 80% of the curriculum in K-12 has no useful application in the workplace.

It seems educators have never performed a *Needs Assessment*. If they had, most of the curriculum would be seen useless in the work places. Filling the school hours with questionable trivia would seem harmless if grades, promotions, and graduation requirements weren't so seriously enforced.

Dr. William H. Easton[1] said: *Education is not a vital factor. Many highly trained persons are sterile creatively, while others accomplish outstanding results in spite of an almost total lack of personal instruction.*

Albert Einstein said: *Faraday's[2] epoch-making discoveries were audacious mental creations which we owe chiefly to the fact that Faraday never went to school, and therefore preserved the rare gift of thinking freely.*

Essential and vital curriculums: reading, writing and basic arithmetic, are the skills upon which students should be graded and upon which employers should do their hiring.

---

[1] Book: *Thinking and how to develop it*. New York. American Society of mechanical engineering, 1946

[2] Faraday: Discovered: Magnetic lines of force, electric motors, Electronic capacitors, and many other electronic devices.

Other subjects such as: geography, health, history, civics, and art should be considered *nice-to-know,* but not essential, and definitely not used for grading.

Subjects such as: trigonometry, advanced algebra, geometry, calculus, science and biology should *never* be taught in public schools, but rather reserved for college courses—for that small cadre of students (less than two percent of the society) who may be embarking on professional careers that require such expertise.

With removal of higher math from public school curriculums, our educational systems could be more focused, far less expensive and of greater benefit to the society. The dropout rate would also be greatly reduced.

Empathy

Empathy—the sum total of our lives' experiences—forms our: insights, attitudes, beliefs, cognizance, and ambitions. As such, it cannot be taught or learned after the fact.

Teachers with their high IQs have never experienced the academic struggles and ineptitudes experienced by low IQ students, and therefore cannot empathize with low achieving students.

Lacking such empathy, teachers have difficulty framing their teaching to fit the understanding of such students.

And being left-brain dominant, teachers are convinced that by enumerating facts and knowledge—

in precise and adopted progression—is adequate. And that the underachiever's lack of comprehension is attributed to: inattention, lack of effort, indifference, and the like.

Needs assessment

In the 50s, Jet aircrafts with Ultra High Frequency Transceivers were being introduced into the Air Defense Command.

I was assigned to set up a school for teaching the UHF equipment.

With a free hand I designed a teaching concept I called: *Means to the end*

I first defined the end requirements and then designed ways and means of obtaining those results.

I believe teachers should first present a need for the subject matter being presented, and then lead the discussion toward the solution.

A Teaching Example

Here's an example for an elementary grade level class: *Students, we need to put up a 40-foot pole to hold a television Antenna. And to keep the pole from being blown down we need to buy wires to go from the top to 4 points on the ground, 30 feet from the bottom of the pole. Question: how many feet of wire should we buy?*

We draw a 4-foot vertical line on the board representing the 40-foot pole, and a slant line from the top to a point 3 feet from the bottom (representing the 30 feet).

We measure the slant line and find it to be 5 feet—deducing this to be 50 feet of wire.

A comment: *This 3-4-5 triangle is used in many professions to insure perfect right angles. We find that by multiplying each length's times themselves, we get: 3x3 + 4x4 = 5x5.*

We can assign letters to represent these three multiples, and use this equation to find the length of any slant line of a triangle with a square corner.

Incidentally, 3,000 years ago a chap discovered this relationship, and wrote the equation: $A^2 + B^2 = C$ His name was Pythagoras. So we call this the Pythagorean theorem.

The Bell Curve

Richard J. Herrnstein and Charles Murray[1] toured the nation's K-12 schools, examining test results on a variety of subjects, and plotted the results on a graph. They found the distribution of scores resembled the classic Bell curve[2].

---

[1] 1 Richard J. Herrnstein & Charles Murray. *The Bell Curve*. Free Press (1994)

[2] A Gaussian distribution named after Karl Gaus.

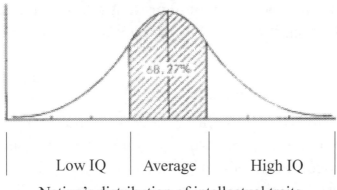

| Low IQ | Average | High IQ |

Nation's distribution of intellectual traits

Nearly half our students fall below the average intelligence level. With teachers lacking communicative skills needed for educating under-achievers, the pathetic results are self-evident.

Under-achieving students are made to feel inferior, and unqualified for holding well paying jobs. They are also candidates for the dropout statistics.

Two approaches might be considered:

1). Certain students that struggle with formal academia and failed to achieve grade level averages above "C" might be selected for cross training, and given teacher status.

These special teachers would certainly be capable of empathizing and communicating effectively with our 50% underachieving students.

Of course, integrating these teachers into the educational process would present a formidable task.

Segregating under-achieving students into *special classes* would not be wise. These special teachers could teach subjects of a complex nature and have students of all intellectual levels in attendance.

Highly intelligent students would not be shortchanged, but would rather be exposed to enhanced academia with associated substance. The material would be presented more pragmatically, and decidedly more memorably.

2). Although our highly intelligent teachers lack empathy with under-achievers, they **might** acquire a *quasi empathy*.

Just as great actors are required to study and acquire the persona of the character they're portraying on the stage or screen, teachers could—through special theatrical training—acquire *quasi empathy*.

And just as great actors require constant coaching, these newly trained teachers could benefit from periodic coaching and monitoring.

College entrance

There's no reason why students with below-average intelligence should be discriminated against when it comes to college admissions.

Just as there's no justification for patronizing highly intelligent students toward educational excellence.

Walk through the awe-inspiring college campuses and gaze upon the luxurious facilities and accouterments.

Then try to explain *why* children born to wealthy, intelligent parents should be the only ones to partake of such tax supported luxuries.

Of course, unlimited enrollment would present accommodation problems. Several remedies come to mind:

- Hold classes in portable classrooms.
- Hold classes 24 hours a day.
- Limit 12 credit hours per semester.
- Limit students to one major
- Limit students to one advanced degree.

Here again, *needs assessment* should be performed to determine exactly which curriculums are actually needed in the work place.

Colleges should not be rigged to fail lower-intelligent students, and to furtively identify the intellectual levels of each of the students.

No child left behind

When politicians get hold of bell ringers, they tend to beat their proud mottos to death. Like motherhood and apple pie: *No Child Left Behind* has an ear-catching ring.

If only this phrase meant what it implies.

In truth, the Executive Order directed states to implement programs that would further denigrate children with below-average intelligence.

More academic testing does, indeed, ingratiate students of higher intelligence, and serves to rally the elite intellectuals.

But it does little to save the children who're always been left behind.

Saving our lost children has a *snowball's-chance-in-hell* of ever becoming part of our nation's landscape.

Tealeaves clearly show a perpetuation of the solution offered by Dr. Edward Teller (nuclear scientist)—in response to USSR's Sputnik victory.

He told President Eisenhower we need to identify students with superior intelligence and construct special programs to accelerate their academic prowess.

At the time of Dr. Tellers' recommendations the USA already had more PhD's than all other nation put together.

Gifted students enrolled in these special classes programs experienced serious psychological problems—of superiority and fear of failing to live up to extremely high expectations.

The struggles of the lower-than-average citizens are closely aligned with, and part and parcel to, the struggle between the *haves and the have-nots*.

These disparities are a high priority of our wealthy brothers and sisters and are being sustained by all means possible.

Those blindly rushing head long into greedy conquests seem unaware, or indifferent to history's' predictability.

12.0

Stop Gay Persecution

In an almost ritualistic kind of persecution—reminiscent of the days of the witch-hunts and evil spirits—our people born with abnormal gene configurations are being condemned and persecuted. It's simply ironic that many leaders of these persecutions are defying their own religious doctrine.

The great Master (Jesus) taught his disciples: *For there are eunuchs [homosexuals] who were so born from their mother's womb.*[1] Yet when confronted with undeniable evidence, certain religious zealots persist in condemning and persecuting people who were so born gay from their mother's womb.

Throughout world history, not one person—however wealthy or powerful—has ever been able to alter his or her sexual orientation.

---

[1] Matthew 19:12 From the Judeo/Christian Bible.

Is there a rational answer to why zealots insist that every human can choose his or her sexual orientations?

Yes indeed, there surely is. But one has to understand a basic human phenomenon that very few seem to understand and even fewer accept, when explained.

Dr. Alfred Kinsey developed his "Kinsey Scale" to illustrate that people are neither gay nor heterosexual but somewhere in between. Through *natural selection,* sexual orientation, like any other gene-induced trait distributes as follows:

Kinsey Scale

1. Gay 10%
2. Gay/Bisexual 12%
3. Bisexual 56%
4. Bisexual/Heterosexual 12%
5. Heterosexual 10%

If we plot the nation's distribution of sexual orientation, our results would form a graph resembling the classic Bell curve:

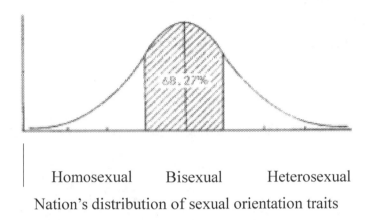

Homosexual   Bisexual   Heterosexual

Nation's distribution of sexual orientation traits

Now back to the rational answer to our perplexing dilemma: Bisexual do, in fact, have a choice (of their sexual preference) and they believe everyone else does as well.

Does this mean zealots (who believe everyone has a choice) are bisexual? Absolutely. For heterosexuals and homosexuals know full well they have no choice.

Most bisexuals are not aware of their bisexuality. Consequently, they don't hesitate to pursue marriages and start families.

Genetically, bisexuals have a very high probability of procreating homosexual children and almost no chance of ever procreating heterosexual children.

The fact that all society's majorities are bisexual and destine to procreate bisexual children is the very reason *older societies*, such as England, France, and Japan, are producing a greater percentage of homosexuals.

If bisexuals were properly diagnosed and instructed, they could resort to alternative methods for building nuclear families, such as:

- Artificial insemination
- Adoption
- In Vitro Fertilization

Laboratories that run sperm banks should be extremely cautious when accepting donors—to be absolutely certain their donors are exclusively and completely heterosexual. The same goes for the harvesting of women's eggs.

Hopefully, in time, our society will be purged of the last of the dark-age curses and be cleansed of this horrific homophobia; will love all mankind, people of all sexual orientations, and will lend support to those so deprived of the sexual traits so many of us take for granted.

13.0

Purge
Our Harmful Laws

Laws against uncontrollable vices invariably lead to crimes that are often worse than the vices.

Uncontrollable vices are those activities that cannot be curbed by laws—such as alcoholic intoxication, prostitution, teen-age smoking, use of narcotics, and gambling.

Perhaps the most glaring example was the 18th Amendment to the Constitution (that prohibited the production and distribution of alcoholic beverages). This amendment led to proliferation of bootlegging and organized crime—of unbelievable proportions.

Outlawing prostitution places the enterprise squarely into the hands of organized crime, and makes it a flourishing and profitable enterprise. Outlawing narcotics trafficking gives organized crime (including street gangs) exclusive control of the ever-burgeoning market.

Illegal gambling would never be so prosperous and widespread if it weren't under control of organized crime syndicates.

Outlawing the sale of cigarettes to minors (the primary source of addiction) makes black-market sales a very profitable enterprise.

Enacting laws against uncontrollable vices merely opens the doors for organized crime and engages expensive and fruitless law enforcement efforts—often with tragic results.

Thousands of narcotics agents have died in vain attempting to enforce un-enforceable narcotics laws.

Solution:

The solution is *not* merely the elimination of these misguided laws. A far more reasonable and logical approach would be for the government to seize control of "uncontrollable vices"—taking them away from organized crime.

This control would not only include government licensing, but also include close monitoring of every facet of the vice. We would also receive taxes presently lost to the underground.

Examples:

1. **Placing prostitution under govt:**
   - Eliminate Streetwalkers.
   - License and inspect Bordellos

- Frequently examine Prostitutes
- Drastically reduce AIDS and VD
- Re-assign officers to real crimes.
- Tax revenues would be recovered.
- Eliminate Serial murders of prostitutes

2. **Place tobacco industry under govt:**
   - Cease tobacco advertisements
   - Remove movie smoking scenes
   - Pack cigarettes in brown wrappers
   - Eliminate cigarette vending machines

3. **Alcoholic-beverages under govt:**
   - Cease alcohol advertising.
   - No alcoholic scenes in movies
   - Alcoholics not in supermarkets
   - Alcoholics in plain containers
   - Warning labels on alcoholics.
   - Warning-message on television.
   - Subsidize Alcoholics rehabilitation

Eliminating unenforceable laws would reduce the embarrassing court cases that squander huge tax dollars and court hours—and fail to achieve any useful purpose.

Instead of squad cars cruising the streets in search of streetwalkers, they could be on the alert for violators of enforceable laws.

Attempts to legislate morality should be seen for the damage such legislations inflict on our society.

Matters of morality should be left to organizations best suited for such endeavors.

When vises such as prostitution are taken over by the government there will be no need for laws against prostitution, and any people duly incarcerated could be exonerate. With prostitution being confined to government-regulated facilities, streetwalkers will be no more.

14.0

Regain
Our Industrial Power

America was once the greatest industrial power in the world. That was before our industries were exported to foreign nations. Now we're dependent, almost entirely, on foreign nations for most of our goods and products. To witness this first-hand, we need merely watch the armada of cargo ships sailing into our harbors and unloading thousands upon thousands of cargo containers.

We soon realize we're no longer producing our own products, and that once again we've become a nation of retailers and farming colonies. Incidentally, even more and more farm products are now being imported.

While millions of workers remain unemployed there seems to be deafening silence in Congress regarding the raping of our American industries.

In fact, to the contrary, we hear endless pontification of the "Fair Trade policies."

With most of our corporations manufacturing products in foreign countries, there's a continual lobbying effort for zero import tariffs against their imports.

This is what they call *Fair Trade*. Very little product-manufacturing capability remains in America, except, of course, for new houses and non-exportable businesses. A nation that loses its' product-producing capability loses its foundation for survival.

We're now dependent on foreign nations for most of our needs, and for bond sales.

The famous economist John Adams predicted that nations that depend solely upon farming, would, by nature, suffer devastating famines every seven years. Our nation presently has about the same amount of manufacturing activity as it did during the Great Depression.

The difference is that we're now surviving on a concept called "leaf raking." This is a concept I learned in Economics 101. The concept goes like this:

Leaf Raking Theory

When great numbers of workers have no jobs, the government hires them to rake leaves to the far end of a large field and pays them each a dollar a day.

The following day the workers come back and rake leaves to the other end of the field. Again they are paid a dollar each. This procedure is repeated every day until the moneys earned re-start the economy and the workers are called back to their real jobs.

Circa 1934, President Franklin D. Roosevelt used this concept in the "New Deal," in which millions of workers were gainfully employed in: WPA (Work Project Administration), and the CCC (Civil Conservation Corp). These programs are but a few examples of numerous leaf-raking projects.

Unless our industries are returned to our country, our entire economy could fall like a house of cards.

To grasp the full significance of this Leaf Raking theory I had to understand the LEVER theory. When a worker spends a dollar, the merchant keeps a nickel and spends the 95 cents. The recipient of the 95 cents keeps a nickel, and spends 90 cents. And so the process continues until the last nickel is spent. Summing up, we find that over ten dollars have been spent and 20 people are five cents richer (for each dollar spent).

This demonstrates how consumer spending can nourish the economy, even though no products are being produced.

The message, of course, is that for each dollar put into circulation ten dollars are added to the economy.

Not too apparent is the fact our economy can *appear* to be prospering even though nothing is being accomplished.

Unfortunately, the preponderance of our economy is derived from *leaf-raking* activities; such as: military defense; retail sales; sales of used products; maintenance and repairs; all government operations; food sales; and healthcare.

Incidentally, the lever effect also works in the opposite direction. When a dollar is taken out of circulation (not spent) it actually removes ten dollars from the economy.

We saw this in 1981 when President Reagan removed 30 billion dollars from entitlements—which essentially lost 300 billion dollars from our economy. Our nation dropped into its worst economic slump since the Great Depression of 1929.

Economy Stimulators

Putting sizable sums of money into the hands of consumers would—in theory—increase consumer spending and ultimately increases manufacturing production—supposedly leading to higher employment, etc. etc.

Seven fallacies in the 2008 cash incentive:

1. lmost all the incentive money was used to pay down credit-card debt. This pays for products already purchased—not more products.

2. Money in the hands of merchants does not buy new products, spur production, or increase employment.
3. Moneys spent on merchandise will actually go to foreign producers, from whence come most of the products.
4. Tight money—with insecure employment—won't be used for high price items such as automobiles.
5. Left over money will go into the bank, or other investments, where it will not be used to stimulate the economy.
6. Foreign production will have no incentive to increase production since little of the incentive money will be spent on imported goods.
7. With few manufacturing facilities in the US, chances of reducing unemployment are slim.

Conclusion:

Instead of stimulating the economy, the plan will do little more than drastically increase our national debt. This should make China and other foreign investors happy.

Retrieving our jobs

Circa 2002, Our Labor Unions pushed their demands too far, and corporate giants, in desperation, played their trump card. They moved all our industries to foreign nations—leaving the Unions high and dry.

Unfortunately, The Corporations also took our nation's primary source of income. Manufacturing marketable goods creates monies; like no other enterprise. Retail, investments, defense spending, healthcare, transportation, government, and the like produce no monies. Such enterprises merely recirculate existing monies.

In truth: Our industries were our nations lifeblood. And there is little hope of ever regaining the industrial power—that once made us the wealthiest nation in the world—if our industries are never rebuilt.

Our industries actually grew on the backs of our laborers, using OUR natural resources, OUR nation's police protection, the security of OUR armed forces, OUR electrical power, gas and water, OUR highway infrastructures, railways, air transportation, and telecommunication services. Since all these resources are owned and paid for by WE Americans, that makes us part owners of all corporations.

Resuscitation of our economy is solely dependent on return, <u>or rebuilding</u>, of our industries.

This returning is not only in the best interest of our work force, our national security, and our industrial power, but it just happens to be—believe it or not—the very best condition for our corporate owners.

Labor Unions

Besides corporate America's obsession with greater and greater profits (via cheaper labor) corporations happen to have an even stronger motivation—that of eliminating labor unions.

For the past six decades, unions have been a painful thorn in big businesses' backsides. The number one priority of many corporate owners has been annihilation of Labor Unions.

The very idea that lowly workers can tell egotistic corporate executives how to pay for work done is insulting.

Many millions of workers have been laid off since 2002 and there is no let up in sight. Absurd, but nevertheless true, is the fact since every worker is a profit sources, these layoffs are, indeed, clear cases of *cutting off one's nose to spite one's face.*

To big business, unions are probably more distasteful than bankruptcy.

Union demands are like a slap in the face of big business—or worse.

It's like spitting in their faces. This festering animosity stems from humongous egos.

Extreme wealth does, indeed, breed egotists and oft times vicious plutocrats.

Some may remember when Andrew Carnegie sent armed troopers into Pittsburg steel mills to break up union organizers. Murder trials never followed the killings.

Are Unions necessary?

Just a word about the flip side of unions: In many companies, the workers consistently vote against union organizing. The reasons should be quite evident.

When employees feel they are being well paid, receiving good fringe benefits, and good working conditions, they don't feel the need to confront management—or to pay union dues.

If corporations are so intent on eliminating unions they certainly have the model to do so.

Apparently it hurts some executives terribly to share the company's profits with underlings

One might think that such brilliant minds could see at least a smidgen beyond their noses. Every nickel they pay the help comes back to them fourfold.

In the final analysis, consumer spending is really the very foundation of our nation's economy.

It's the workers' purchases that feed the goose that lays the golden eggs.

In some companies, the employees actually share profit increases. Such companies are not likely to have unions.

Anything that increases employee salaries results in increased sales and greater profits—providing, of course, that the employees have no reason to hold tight to their incomes—such as during the threat of layoffs.

We saw what happened when President Kennedy gave everyone a sizable tax break—at a time when employment was at an all time high and our economy was booming. Sales flourished and government revenues exceeded the national budget.

In fact, many people were so confident in the economy they were out spending their tax windfall long before they received it.

Unfortunately, this practice does not succeed when workers are afraid of losing their jobs and the economy is on the down-slope.

We witnessed this in the 1980s when President Reagan gave the wealthiest top one-percent a humungous tax reduction (from 70% down to 50%).

This attempt failed to offset the damages caused by the cut of 30 billion dollar in entitlements.

Ten million workers lost their jobs, and many car dealers went out of business.

The *well-to-do* seem to suffer grave discomfort when our government doles out money to the poorer class.

They (the well-to-do) fight like tigers to prevent the lower class workers from being granted a living wage; not realizing that the few cents these workers receive all come back fourfold to the well-to-do.

A viable solution would be the retrieving of our pirated industries.

Of course, we should never expect Corporate giants to return our industries if Labor Unions were a part of the equation; even though returned industries would mean elimination of dealing with foreign nations, ocean going shipments, long distance trucking of products, and restoration of the "Made in USA label."

We might hope that our corporate giants will soon tire of their involvement with foreign natives, the ocean going trips, and the complexities of money exchange.

Living and working on American soil has got to be more appealing than committing precious time and energy to foreign nations (?)

Perhaps (Wishful thinking) our Labor Union leaders might see the big picture, offer truce, and become a vital asset in a renewed manufacturing creation.

Retrieving our industries

There are several ways in which we might encourage our industries to return to the USA:

ZERO business taxes. (Businesses don't pay taxes; they merely pass them on to the customers)
ZERO Unions Union leaders would be reimbursed for lost union dues.
ZERO relocation costs
Shipping costs would be reimbursed for returning equipment.
Impose huge import tariffs Import tariffs would be levied on products of American manufacturers
ZERO sale taxes on USA products. Products made in the USA would require no sales tax.

Alternative

If our industries are not returned, then our government will have to build and operate new industries. Not being required to show a profit we could prices commodities very affordable. Employees, being well paid could afford most of the products being manufactured. The government would pay all heath benefits, and typical fringe benefits. Since the public would, in essence, own the industries unions would have no purpose.

15.0

End Our
Nation's Poverty

We solved the poverty problem of other nations merely by sending them our industries. Solvency and wealth of a nation are wholly dependent its manufacturing capabilities. We speak of this in chapter 14 (*Regain Our Industrial Power*). Since there's little likelihood of ever reclaiming our lost industries, we are left with one alternative.

We've got to build new industries. And since new industries, within our borders, would mean a resurgence of more labor union, our *corporate giants* aren't about to build new industries—even though our entire economy stands on the brink of collapse.

With guarded apprehension, I dare mention the dreaded "S" word.

Other nations on the brink of economic disaster have resorted to Socialism.

The greatest obstacle to these other nations has been the tenacious and powerful insurgence from our CIA.

Fear of Socialism gaining favor throughout the world has always posed a threat for our industrial giants. For socialism would seize our industries and give them to the public—such as happened in the 1919 USSR, to Castro's Cuba, and to Vietnam.

With conditions as they are, government-owned industries would pose no competition for the corporate giants. Who no longer have industries here in the USA.

And our US labor market would always be far more expensive than foreign markets.

The primary objective of Government-owned industries would be full employment. With good salaries being earned by an entire employable population we would have an enormous and vibrant consumer market.

Manufactured products would be primarily for citizen use, both necessities and luxuries, but there would also be products for selling to foreign markets.

Income from sales, of course, would all go to the government, deferring the need for most income taxes.

An affluent and fully employed populace would: enjoy minimal crime.

The income could easily pay for improved infrastructures and advanced transportation; could develop educational systems beneficial to all levels of intellect; could provide healthcare for the entire populous; would be a burgeoning consumer market for all the products produced here and abroad, and would build a solid and prosperous economy.

At some point our nation's people need to recognize and accept the prevailing gradation of the mass's skills and mentalities. Viewing all people with the *one-size-fits-all* mentality borders on the blindsided, and smacks of cruel indifference.

We can scoff at socialist policies *nurturing the inept and unmotivated,* but at least the *unemployables,* when salaried, do contribute to the consumer base.

If we continue to discourage efforts to reduce procreations of mentally inept, and mentally challenged, our consciences will continue to be fraught with veiled guilt.

16.0

Balanced Lobbying

When you go to Washington, D. C. to visit your representatives, where do you suppose they are?

They're probably not in the legislative chambers. They seldom are. They're more likely in their offices, meeting with large campaign contributors; being briefed on proposed bills.

Thousands of professional lobbyists form the source and nucleus of our nation's law—creation system. In essence, this is the mainstay of our government.

Allegedly, our representatives are elected to serve the public—not special interests.

This is not to imply that bills offered by special interest groups are undesirable to the general public.

Some such bills may well serve the best interest of the masses.

When legislators consider bills note worthy, they should share the essence of the bill with those that'll be affected, and be aware of the wishes of those affected.

Before a bill is debated, the names of the author, lobbyist, and origin of the bill should be announced on the floor of the legislator.

Ground rules

To level the playing field, and provide a means for the masses to have their needs and wishes made known, our representatives should be required to hold Town Meetings in their district on a schedule to be determined.

This should be a standard practice, and a basic responsibility of the people's representative's.

Of course, since campaign contributions from the masses wouldn't begin to compete with those of special interests, the wishes of the masses that oppose the special interest's wishes will normally stand little chance of being proposed in the legislation.

However, the masses do have reprisals. They represent the majority at the polling places. And if their wishes are ignored, they can make such feelings known by informing the masses.

17.0

Save Our Newborn

A fate worse than death, as the saying goes. No, we're not talking abortion. Our next horribly egregious practice has to do with the way our society indiscriminately imposes dreadful life sentences of obesity on more than half of our newborn children.

Obese families know all too well the anguish and torment that overweight people must endure throughout their entire lifetime.

And yet, we seem to have no compunctions when it comes to filling our students' heads with irrelevant trivia, while apparently feeling no guilt when we fail, miserably, to teach our students the most critical facts of life.

We allow our young and old alike to gamble with the lives of children—yet to be conceived—by indiscriminately indulging our sexual appetites, much like cats and dogs.

We can no longer wait for our reluctant medical scientists to admit, and put on record, that obesity is strictly genetic.

Anyone with even a modicum of common sense can see that entire families and their ancestors are undeniably cut from the same cloth.

What sort of parent would place their newborn on a sacrificial altar and bestow upon it a curse of unbearable obesity? But that's exactly what obese people do when they indulge in sexual exploits without birth control. They're playing Russian roulette with human lives.

Am I advocating that obese people should never procreate? Absolutely!!! It's difficult to stand by and observe such recklessness without doing something to prevent such catastrophes.

Many years ago a number of states adopted laws referred to as *eugenics*. These laws mandated that people be sterilized, without their consent, if they carried certain genetic anomalies, such as: insanity (criminal or otherwise).

Abortion was mandatory in cases of rape when the rapist was determined to be criminally insane or when a pregnancy was via incest.

Religious organizations mounted strenuous opposition to any attempts to prevent the propagation of the insane.

The laws were removed from the books and insanity has been proliferating ever since.

It's fully expected that any attempts to curb the proliferation of obesity would be similarly opposed.

Churches depend on population proliferation, by whatever means, and in whatever form, in order to grow and maintain their memberships.

Nonetheless, we should search for some form of obesity prevention—preferably short of legislation.

First and foremost, the primary source of obesity needs to be brought out into the open. Ignorance and stupidity should be replaced with a hefty dose of common sense.

We can no longer wait for medical science to fess up with the truth.

The obesity message needs to *be taught in schools, in seminaries, and in colleges—let it be written in primers, spelling books, and in almanacs;—let it be preached from the pulpits, proclaimed in the legislative halls*[1].

Mating couples should be aware of the mental and physical traits of their offspring's, and should realize just how their off-springs will feel about their parent's perpetration of their physical and mental traits. We frequently hear of children shooting their parents.

---

[1] A paraphrase of Lincoln's address before the Young Men's Lyceum, Springfield, Ill.

Predicting offspring traits

Children should do a prognostic school assignment to forecast their own childbearing prognostics— while still in their pre-puberty years:

1). Draw up one's family tree, tracing parents back to great, great-grandparents.
2). Prepare survey sheets for **each** person on the family tree, as follows:

Name _____
Relation _____
Weight _____
Height _____
Mentality[1] _____

3). Teachers should summarize results of each student's ancestors, and provide each student with their off springs predictability.

Dealing with abnormal predictions

Should we procreate children if obesity, mental problems, genetic anomalies, addictions, physical handicaps, and so on, are prominent in our family tree?

Obese people, alcoholics, gays, physically handicapped, etc. will surely look at their parents at

---

[1]   Normality or abnormality

times, and wonder why their parents inflicted upon them such unbearable curses.

Alternatives:

Genetic anomalies need not deprive parents of the exhilarating experiences of raising children.

There are ways of having nuclear families without risking the lives of newborn.

- Adoption
- Artificial insemination[1]
- In vitro Fertilization[2]

Pregnancy prevention should include effective birth control, or in critical cases, Tubal Ligation[3] for the female or vasectomy for the male. Prevention, however, is only part of the solution.

It's only natural that people desire, very strongly, a family with children—regardless of their physical size and weight.

Adoption has proven extremely successful for millions of families and should definitely be a serious consideration.

But for some, carrying a child in their own womb is nothing short of thrilling fulfillment. Anything

---

[1] Donated sperm is injected up the birth canal
[2] Ovum is fertilized in a glass
[3] Tying off the fallopian tubes

short of this might be less than satisfactory. In such cases the test-tube baby might be acceptable.

For *In vitro Fertilization*, and *Artificial Insemination*, it is super-critical that the ovum and sperm be harvested from heterosexual, non-obese donors.

If the woman's family happens to be uniformly slender and the husband's family predominantly obese, then artificial insemination might be sufficient. Here again, the source of sperm must be very carefully selected.

With strong emphasis on obesity prevention, specialty laboratories should be created with foolproof methods of harvesting acceptable ova, and sperm banks should be established and carefully controlled.

Our emphasis needs to be focused on the potential child, not the needs and wishes of prospective parents. As a highly civilized people we need to ensure that every newborn child is given a fighting chance, as well as every opportunity we can provide.

If all this sounds like Hitler's idea of a master race, then you've missed the whole point. An overwhelming population of huge overweight people with the potential for numerous health risks need not inhabit our society.

Our 60 million-plus obese people are essentially a lost cause—genetically controlled metabolism being unalterable.

But we certainly can do something about the next generation.

Weight Reduction

Body fat is actually stored excess nutrition. Overactive metabolisms absorb more nutrition than required, and the surplus is stored throughout the body. This absorption takes place in our small intestines.

If digested food is sped through the small intestines before full absorption can take place, then nutrient absorption will be lessened.

If the absorption is less than the body requires for a given period of time, then the body will extract from stored nutrition (body fat)—causing a reduction in body weight.

Speeding digested foods through the small intestines may be done in a number of ways.

- Daily use of prunes and prune juice
- Laxatives (including Metamucil)
- Fruits and vegetables
- Eliminate pastries and red meats
- Drink non-fat milk
- Walk, swim or run twice a week
- Drink six glasses of water daily

Note: Addictive anorexia is a mental disease affecting less than one percent of the population, and not the result of the using the above means of expediting the flow of digested foods.

Speeding digested foods through the small intestines, is an excellent regimen for obese people, and does not deprive one of the necessary nutrients. Metabolisms will absorb adequate nutrients.

If concerns or doubts arise, a doctor's care might be advisable.

18.0

Ethnic Blending

Commendable progress has been made in our melding of the races. We can certainly take pride in the numerous triumphs that have come our way.

Races of all colors—white, brown, red, and yellow—revere and idolize and even sometimes love our black athletes, entertainers, politicians, scholars, physicians, and executives; living proof that whites do not genetically hate or even dislike all blacks.

And if that's not sufficient, let's witness the hundreds (maybe thousands) of interracial marriages and love affairs.

What then are the lingering undercurrents that manifest in many forms of hatred? Their definitely are unprovoked animosities in most venues. And such animosities do, indeed, stand in the way of a national unification.

In our attempts to identify the root causes of such divisiveness, we'll step back, shed all forms of bias and prejudice, and begin our search.

This quest takes me back to my early childhood. I was two or three years old. One of the older kids in the neighborhood told me if I called a black man the "N" word he would cut my throat. While standing, safely, behind my front-yard fence and being devilishly confrontational, I waited until a black man was passing by and I shouted the "N" word and dashed into the house.

This story is not to illustrate how prejudice is formed, but rather to trace the formulation of prejudices. This older boy did not form this opinion by himself. Children invariably emulate their parents and take pride in mimicking them.

Even the parents were probably not the origin of bias. Adults circulate opinions, and hatred is passed down from generation to generation. And hatred often feeds upon itself.

We'd be grossly unfair to place the source of racial bias on either race, but to trace the evolution we would be judicious to look at the situations from both sides.

Plantation owners feared for their lives—partly from their guilt of abusive treatment and partly from being greatly out-numbered.

As a means of gaining some sense of security, owners decided to promulgate religious beliefs. Feeling that the fear of God would prevent the risk of insurrection.

The omnipresent fear, however, continued to permeate the South and tended to put all white people on their guard when in the vicinity of blacks.

In their efforts to build barriers, the whites invoked severe restrictions as to the use of public facilities and transportation.

This fear has lingered on through the centuries, although it has somewhat mitigated.

Years of belittlement, segregation, and just downright dislike have undoubtedly etched deep-seated resentment and suspicions against the whites.

These feelings are reflected on somber masks that seem on guard against challenging smiles and nods from opposite races.

People on both sides—especially introverts—go about in fear of receiving a nasty *screw you* or a verbal *drop dead* response, if they dare give a friendly greeting or a pleasant smile—to a perfect stranger.

On-the-job relationships can be exceptions to these reactions and can contribute wonderfully to ameliorating such on-guard situations.

In spite of lingering overtures, more and more people—all colors—are experiencing spine-tingling thrills when they dare confront a somber appearance with courageous smiles, or cheerful howdy do's.

Like breaking the ice, one enjoyable encounter can lead to more of the same; and before long a person feels comfortable and even enjoys greeting one of the opposite race.

The question still remains: how do we bring prevailing resentments and mistrust into the same pleasant experiences that many (definitely not a majority) are enjoying?

Since we can unanimously agree that racial bias is not genetic and that we've witnessed endless cases of remarkable conversions, we can also agree that conversion is not impossible in the great majority of cases.

What immediately comes to mind is a need to bring the numerous conversions—along with their wonderful rewards—to the attention of those in waiting.

We've already witnessed untold opportunities, in the thousands of movies, television shows, and other media.

Unbelievably exciting friendships have been vividly portrayed and no one can deny the tremendous spiritual and humanistic interactions such relationships can provide.

However, all this positive exposure has not completely eradicated the deep-seated distrust and anxiety that prevails—usually disguised, and in guarded pretense.

Two possibilities come to mind:

1) Our President and revered leaders (including clergy) could initiate challenges to encourage all whites to make a concerted effort to greet black people with a loving smile and, if possible, a friendly greeting.
2) Highly publicize success stories in which blacks and whites worked together, and depended on each other under trying circumstances.

While this, my Forth Edition, was in the re-write and editing phase, Barack Obama was elected president—opening an amazing and wonderful chapter in the annals of ethnicities.

It might be interesting to know how he was elected. The Republicans were horrified that Hillary would be nominated and run away with the presidential election. They pulled out all the stops and spent obscene amounts of money to nominate Obama—confident that he (Obama) could never be elected.

19.0

Restrain Our
Competitive Craze

As long as we're endeavoring to make our wonderful nation as great as it can be, we would do well to own up to one of our most heinous indiscretions—that of fostering hatred through competitive sports. Who would believe that America's revered sports are actually contributing to our society's hatred, animosity, and in some cases even crime?

Next to *apple pie and motherhood*, our sports fanaticism ranks near the top of our list of idolatries. This reverence blinds us to its devastating effects such as the Columbine massacres. I'm afraid, that revealing this aspect of sports might be like revealing a long held family secret.

Sit in the bleachers at any Little League game and observe how some of the parents are teaching our children one of their most damaging lessons.

These lessons are carried over to virtually every competitive sport on and off the playgrounds.

At times we actually witness parents inflicting bodily harm, and in one case death (at a hockey practice).

Many of us probably remember our own parents' unsportsmanlike conduct in the stands, and wonder how these behaviors may have affected our own combatant attitudes.

The compulsion to win—at any cost—is an integral part of every team sport—from children's sports, to high school competitions to college athletics, and on up to professional sports.

Coach Vince Lombardi's famous motto: *Winning isn't everything, it is the only thing,* clearly implies that good sportsmanship, excellent performance, and persistence in the face of adversity mean nothing.

Football is one sport (second only to boxing in the quest for the title of most barbaric) in which the object is to inflict as much physical punishment on the opposition as possible.

Kill the quarterback is more than a figurative expression.

Defensive linemen who succeed in maiming and putting quarterbacks out of the game are applauded as the teams' heroes.

I well remember the time my football coach switched me from fullback to tackle and said that to remain on the team I had to be willing to knock the opponents senseless.

Brutally attacking a stranger who has done me no harm didn't seem the way civilized people should treat each other.

So I opted out and joined our school band. I'm sure that athletically inclined students can find less barbaric forms of release and gratification.

The drive to win, leads opponents into combatant positions, and by definition, to become rivals. It's virtually impossible to compete without harboring some resentment toward our competitors. And resentment invariably contaminates the soul.

Sports arenas, of course, are not the only place humans vent their insatiable quest for victory. Winning can be the coveted prize in: road rage, occupational promotions, card games, chess, parlor games, quiz shows, and the list goes on. Competition in any form tends to breed hostility and distrust.

Field and track events do have an element of competition, but less defiant are the confrontations that infect other sports. The audience receives a brain rush every time a record is broken—regardless of which athletes break the records.

Admittedly, there is the team's will to win.

One unfortunate and somewhat shameful disappointment in Olympics competitions is the pitting of nation against nation. It's the ole: *Us against them attitude.*

Why couldn't the objective be for athletes to strive for record scores, without reference to countries? Athletes could wear the uniforms specific for each event.

Ted Turner was provoked by the Olympic rivalry, and staged the largest private Olympiad in history—the $100 million Goodwill Games in Moscow. Metals were not awarded to nations.

Business giants have long touted competition as the lifeblood of industrial progress, even when it leads to cutthroat destruction of competing companies, the ruination of organized unions, and the exporting of entire industries to foreign countries.

A valuable product, well made, reasonably priced and conveniently available is its own best competition. Insatiable greed masquerading as healthy competition is not an absolute necessity.

Mr. Milton S. Hershey developed a delicious chocolate and built the largest chocolate company in the world, when there was no significant competition.

He built a wealthy home/school—over a hundred luxury homes—for about 2,000 disenfranchised children at a time. The Home now owns controlling shares in the corporation, worth over six billion dollars.

When competition is little more than *a dog eat dog* sort of rivalry, it needs to be recognized for what it really is—a shameful force of evil and an infectious sickness that attacks our civility and creates a breeding ground for social mistrust, hatred, and festering animosities.

Oh yes. We hear that competition is the force that motivates improvement and fosters a desire for excellence—and so it does.

The movie "Miracle on 43rd Street" illustrated an interesting paradigm: two giant department stores helping each other make Christmas a most profitable experience—Fiction, of course—but for great minds, certainly worth contemplation.

We greatly enjoy ice shows, such as the Ice Capades and the Ice Follies in which each skater attempts to perform his or her very best, hoping to thrill and entertain paying audiences.

Figure Skaters don't compete against each other. They compete against a score sheet. Audiences have their favorites, but generally seek thrilling performances from all skaters.

Wouldn't it be wonderful if we could replace angry competition—particularly brutal sports like boxing and football—with superb athletic performances?

In a utopian society, sports would only involve athletic events in which people, working and playing together, would attempt to perform exceptional feats of speed, strength, and beauty.

At no time would it be necessary for people or teams to be pitted against each other. Am I a dreamer? Yes. But isn't that what makes the world go round—and a better world in which to live?

When citizen work together to build organizations, public facilities, public parks, homes for the homeless, and such, to give the masses fruitful enjoyable lives, good health, and friendships, our existence takes on new meaning and creates the foundation for a Far, Far Better America.

20.0

Attack Crime
At its Roots

How can a crime-ridden nation in clear conscience claim greatness? Crime ranks next to death, divorce, and illness in fears threatening our society.

In dealing with crime, our law enforcers almost invariably limit their emphasis to capture, conviction and confinement. Unfortunately, *crime prevention* is conspicuous by its absence.

Prevention seems elusive, and something our public officials seem unwilling, unable or incapable of engaging.

Police are quick to point out that they cannot respond until a crime has been committed. Some people feel that inundating our communities with large numbers of police will discourage criminal activities.

This begs the real question, since crimes are rarely committed on the streets or in the byways.

If we truly seek crime prevention we must attack the root causes.

We need to know why people commit crimes. Of course, we can all recite numerous reasons, but if we're to find ways of preventing crimes, we need to delve more deeply into situations and conditions that lead to these numerous reasons.

If a person steals bread to feed his starving family, we first need to ask: why doesn't this man have the wherewithal to buy bread?

And if the answer is: he has no job, we need then to find out why. If there are no jobs to be had, then again we need ask: why.

People who have the drive and the smarts to commit crimes surely have enough initiative and savvy to hold a good job.

Perhaps it goes without saying that our crime rate increases as our unemployment rate increases. This being the case, then why do officials slough off unemployment statistics as just another routine statistic?

People in authority seem to quote unemployed numbers like they're giving the weather reports.

Not only are the millions of unemployed people living in dire straights, but our nation is also suffering.

With unemployment comes reduced consumer power, as well as reduced state and federal revenues.

Plus, the government is required to pay out huge sums of unemployment compensation.

People who hold down good jobs and can afford food, clothing, and shelter (plus cars, vacations and entertainment) would hardly jeopardize such enviable life styles by venturing into criminal activities.

On the other hand, people who can't afford minimal necessities and may be facing life-threatening conditions may feel they have nothing to lose and much to be gained—should they be caught in the commission of a crime.

At least they'd be provided food, clothing, and shelter, while being incarcerated.

We could list numerous reasons for the lack of jobs, but no reasons can begin to compare with the fact that most of our industrial jobs have been shipped overseas and there are few substantial jobs to be had.

When we hear politicians talk about creating more jobs, we immediately recognize we're hearing frivolous platitudes.

And that only a thin shred of possibility lies in the creation of bottom-feeding jobs.

Service and sales jobs do not produce products, add to our nation's industrial power, or secure our economy.

Many jobs, good jobs, can and will be created if only we do what's necessary to rebuild our industries' base.

Elsewhere in this thesis (Section 14. *Regain Our Industrial Power*) we proposed ways and means of doing just that.

But there is more we need to address. Still on the law books are laws prohibiting businesses from buying out their competitors. These laws were put in place to prevent companies from amassing powerful monopolistic powers and endangering the nation's economic diversity (a justification for socialism).

A collateral danger is the creation of uncontrollable monopolistic empires. Hundreds of competing enterprises have been gobbled up by humungous (and illegal) conglomerates—while ignoring the loss of millions of jobs. And here we're talking primarily about retail enterprises, not manufacturing corporations.

During 1992 to 1999 we had the lowest unemployment rate (4.5%) since 1920.

To enable every American to acquire comfortable lifestyles, we need to make the creation of good sound jobs (in manufacturing facilities) our nation's *number one priority*.

Unemployment above 5.0% should signal a national crisis and should call for a state of emergency.

To deal with such an emergency we should be willing to: jeopardize a fraction of our gigantic military budget; levy large import tariffs on products made by American companies, and drastically cut back on moneys *loaned* to foreign nations.

It probably wouldn't hurt to confine our space missions to ground based research.

Bringing industries into the USA should not be a political football, but should be held as the lifeblood of our nation's economical survival and the creation of a crimeless society.

Crime is much like illness. We don't become overly concerned until we—or someone we know—become a victim. How fantastic it would be if we, or those we know, were to go through life without ever falling prey to a crime. We certainly hope and pray we never will.

To provide crime-prevention, we need to re-store the *Great Industrial Power* that once was ours.

Unless we take action soon, our nation will continue down its slippery slope toward a frightening abyss, where powerful greedy billionaires will reign like kings, and depression will hit like a tornado.

Merely locating and elevating the right leader to the White House will set the stage for retrieving our government.

For the sake of the ruling tycoons, let's hope their insatiable greed doesn't inflame some sort of ghastly insurrection. Even our downtrodden and poverty-ridden millions don't wish for that to happen.

21.0

Unify our Foundation

There was a time when all our children were homogeneously merged into our society by spending thirteen years mingling, confronting, and socializing with a huge slice of Americana.

Our children's journey into the outside world was paved with foresight and preparation. Even as parents we tasted of the mix of friends being brought home—occasionally shocking surprises.

But that was then. Now, we're in a quandary of divisiveness. We have: charters schools; religious schools; home schools; private schools; magnum schools; and who knows what new break-away may be lurking on the horizon.

Loss of social solidarity may not be the worst harm. These divisions—into fraternal like elements—must certainly be developing leagues of consorting relationships between separately schooled students.

This divisiveness has deep and consorted origin. Throughout history, there's been a natural compulsion—stemming from *survival of the fittest*—motivating the ***fittest*** to acquire control and ownership over entire realms, and to absorb all that possessions have to offer.

Vast acquisitions encourage and increase cravings for control of more and more possessions.

Fittest populations—comprised almost exclusively of intellectual elites—do what comes naturally. With their superior intelligence they build and protect their coveted turf.

To perpetuate their scholarly vigilance and to be sure of their established environment, they retain control of the educational system and set the standards to ingratiate the intellectual element, while subjugating and controlling the lower class of students.

This insures exclusive post-graduate intellects, and selective inculcation into privileged employment opportunities.

If all this discourse sounds like a denunciation or castigation of the intellects, it's not that at all! Anyone who might've been born with high levels of intellectual genes would naturally do exactly the same.

This does bring to mind, however, a piece de resistance.

Our genes do, in fact, determine innate intelligence, and our ancestry happens to be the source of our genes.

Our overwhelming need to procreate our own bloodline takes precedence over any attempts to control our genes. This indeed, is Mother Nature at her best.

Any breeding schemes aimed at procreating the most intelligent; the healthiest; the best looking; the most physically agile, and mentally adept children might certainly be inferred as a Hitler-type scheme—for breeding the *master race*.

However, women who use *in vitro fertilization* do have choice of both sets of genes being implanted.

Women using Artificial Insemination have a choice of male genes being contributed. To this extent, people having unfavorable traits can, indeed, procreate children free of such traits.

We mention, in chapter 17 (*Save our New Born*), several ways in which we can prevent the procreating of obese children.

Preventing our children from inheriting unfavorable traits should not be considered attempts to promote the *master race*.

Many believe our intelligence can be improved via proper training. Like any trait, it can be exercised and kept alert, but the innate intelligence gene is unalterable.

A person born with an IQ of 70 will retain that level throughout his or her life. And such a person's offspring will be genetically influenced accordingly.

Of course, both partners do influence the inheritance gene pool, and the composite results are not precisely predictable.

But hoping that a partner with good intelligence genes will make up for the partner with poor intelligence genes is playing Russian roulette with a child's life.

Running the risk of procreating a child with low intelligence disregards the probability that such a child will have to endure this throughout his or her life.

We've alluded to the advantages experienced by children with high levels of intelligence. They live in an entirely different world.

In the past, this knowledge was not well accepted, and the populous went about procreating children with intelligence-level distributions resembling the classic Bell curve.

Suggesting a system for procreating children with high levels of intelligence is by no means the purpose of this text.

But people in search of marital mates should definitely keep such thoughts upper-most in their minds.

In chapter 17 (Save Our Newborn) we offer much food-for-thought on this subject.

Returning to the proliferation of school types—a condition possibly beyond rectification—common sense and a stroke of conscience might see things as they should be, and dare bring our public schools to the prominence for which they are sorely needed.

No other element in our society has as high an intrinsic value as our public schools.

22.0

Marriages
To be avoided

In recent years the marriage phenomenon has begun to take center stage. Horrific debates are becoming commonplace. Meanwhile, our divorce rate is rising above 50%.

Many, if not most, marriages are doomed from the start—through no fault of either partner. The threat lies in differences between certain gene-controlled traits. These differences are often undetected until well into the marriage.

We know that our genes determine our eye and hair color, blood type, skin color, height, facial appearances, etc. But until recently, medical science has not been willing to acknowledge that certain other traits are gene controlled and unalterable.

Such traits are: personality, intelligence, sexual orientation, and sexual appetite.

Our mental and physical traits fall on a scale somewhere between two extremes—with about 60% of the population falling near the middle third of each of the trait spectrums.

If couples contemplating marriage have any of the following traits falling on widely separated points on their respective spectrums, chances of sustaining permanent marriages are unfavorable:

- Sexual orientation
- Sexual appetites
- Personality
- Innate intelligence

Sexual Orientation

We're all born with genes that determine exactly where we fall on the sexual-orientation spectrum. Proof of this can be seen from the fact that no one—however wise, powerful, or wealthy—has ever been able to alter their sexual orientation one iota.

If such alteration had ever been achieved it would've gone down in history as one of the greatest achievements of all times.

Homosexuals the world over would devote their life to acquiring the formula for such alteration.

About 60% of the population fall in the middle third of the scale and would be classified as bisexual. Another 20% falls somewhere along the heterosexual end of the scale and about 20% fall somewhere along the homosexual end of the scale.

These percentages are approximations based on natural selection, statistical probabilities, and observable intuition. They're cited here for illustrative purposes.

Heterosexuals find thoughts of same-sex involvement repulsive, while homosexuals find thoughts of opposite-sex repulsive. And of course, bisexuals have no strong preferences one-way or the other.

We can loosely divide bisexuals into three sub-categories:

1) Those who prefer opposite-sex, but don't find same-sex repulsive,
2) Those who prefer same-sex, but wouldn't find opposite-sex repulsive, and
3) Those—in dead center—who have equal preference for both.

We occasionally hear about *homosexuals* who—through some *special therapy*—are able to change their orientation (to that of heterosexual).

This overlooks the probabilities of bisexuality and their freedom of choice.

Bisexuals, especially those near the middle of the scale, with their dual-preferences, are at liberty to go in either direction and may change their relationships at will. Their innate orientation, however, remains unaffected.

Most bisexuals are unaware of these classifications. They, unlike heterosexuals and homosexuals (who have clear preferences) generally spend much of their life attempting to put their sexual feelings into perspective—torn between societies' highly polarized bias and their own natural instincts.

It's not uncommon, now days, to hear about wives who discover their husband's are having extra marital relationships—with other men.

Many bisexuals hope marriage will cure their homosexual tendencies. They endure a less than desirable relationship in an opposite-sex marriage—as long as they can.

Eventually, they surrender to their natural urges—often procreating a child or two in the process.

Homosexual spouses, desiring to be with their lovers, usually instigate the divorces.

The most tragic outcome of such failures is the procreation of homosexual children.

Offspring's resulting from such ill-gotten marriages will forever be subjected to the abuse and inhuman castigation dealt by an ignorant society.

These children will never feel the thrill, excitement and fulfillment of falling in love with a person of the opposite sex; conceiving children in the holiness of marriage and raising those children in a traditional heterosexual environment.

Oh yes, in years to come, a more enlightened and more benevolent society will condone, and perhaps even bless, the forming of sexual bonds between those of the same gender.

An informed society will also come to realize that children cannot be persuaded to become homosexuals by homosexual teachers or guardians—blocking child adoption by united-homosexual partners.

Also, in this more benevolent society, people needn't conform to life styles alien to their natural feelings.

Bisexuals need to be appraised of the futility of using marriage to solve their genetic anomaly. And our society needs to rise above its dark-age mentality.

Sexual Appetites

Most of us are born with average-sexual appetites, that is; mid way on the sexual-appetite spectrum; a spectrum that extends from sexual disinterest (virtual frigidity) at one end to insatiable craving on the opposite end.

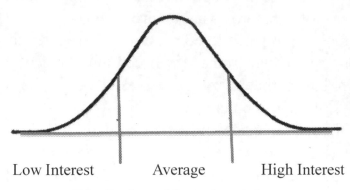

Low Interest   Average   High Interest

Distribution of Sexual appetites

During the courting phase, the excitement of discovering another person's attractiveness and the returned admiration; along with the newness of exploring another person's physical uniqueness often over shadows any objective awareness of our new-acquaintance's genetic traits.

The aura that marriage creates is in itself a magic elixir; it can transport new friendships into a sort of euphoria.

Significant differences in sexual appetites may not become apparent until the newness of a marriage begins to wane.

Years into the marriage, differences in sexual appetites begin to plague the couple's sexual encounters.

The spouse with the larger appetite will sense a growing frustration and sexual craving, while the spouse with the lesser appetite will sense a growing annoyance and will begin to find the perpetual advances from his or her partner somewhat uncouth and perhaps perverted.

The frustrated spouse is likely to seek sexual gratification outside the marriage, and before long the marriage is doomed.

Note: Many *Perfectly matched* spouses— according to Kinsey and Masters and Johnson—have extra-marital involvements without endangering the marriage.

Introvert/Extrovert

The expression: *Irreconcilable differences*, is a name often given to marital conflicts that can't be accurately identified. Frequently, the problem is really a *personality conflict* with one spouse nearer the introvert end, and the other nearer the extrovert end.

Here again, such difference are obscure during the honeymoon phase and don't impact the relationship until the newness begins to wear off.

Even then, the animosities, which surface, are rarely identified as personality differences. The cause is often attributed to, "falling out of love."

We recognize introvert and extrovert behavior in others—particularly in public places. In a restaurant, for example, the load voice of the extrovert is readily apparent, while the timid soft-spoken introvert is not so obvious.

We're not so keenly aware of such differences in our own spouse's personality, even though they may lie at the source of our marital problems. In fact, the imposing prominence of a strong extrovert may be the very feature that attracted the shy introvert in the first place.

During periods of anxiety and tiredness, the piercing, grating sound of the boisterous extroverted spouse can be overbearing, especially for spouses that are inclined towards the introverted persuasion. Conversely, extroverts tend to be irritated and intolerant of spouses who are withdrawn and maudlin.

These differences often become prominent in social circles where the extrovert feels compelled to exhibit exuberance and gaiety while the introvert feels embarrassment and longs for the sanctity of the home.

Both behaviors play havoc with the other partner's patience.

Personality test are available that identify the point at which each of the prospective couples fall on the introvert/extrovert scale.

A prospective marriage is headed for trouble if a couple's personality ratings differ significantly.

Intelligence

We're all born with an innate intelligence that is unalterable; that is, our brains have unique cellular configurations, just as do our bodies, and nothing short of brain surgery can alter that configuration.

Of course, we can train our brains to be as effective as possible—just as we train our bodies to be as agile and athletic as possible.

And just as all the physical training in the world could never make us Olympic gold-metal winners, no amount of mental training would make us into intellectual giants, if we don't possess a genius level of innate intelligence.

Intellectual differences, if contemplating marriage, should warn of problems.

Unfortunately, we've yet to develop a valid test of human intelligence.

Current testing attempts are unduly influenced by the need for experience, knowledge, and skills in reading and writing.

Problems arise when highly intelligent spouses attempt to discuss matters with their less-intelligent spouses.

Less-intelligent spouses, attempting to show interest, may offer comments that tend to reveal disinterest or implications that the topic is irrelevant.

Conversely, when the less intelligent spouse is eager to discuss ideas, the more intelligent spouse finds it difficult to give any attention or credibility to such ideas.

Then too, there's a high probability that more intelligent spouses will use their mental superiority to take advantage of the less intelligent spouse, such as: in the distribution of the family wealth, and numerous other competitive matters.

As married couples mature, intelligence tends to occupy a more prominent role, and the lesser spouse may be viewed as a liability.

The more intelligent spouse is likely to seek acquaintances with equal intelligence—with which to share common interests.

While the more intelligent partner is finding fulfillment in newfound relationships, the less intelligent partner is becoming vulnerable to outside associations that promise compassion and understanding.

23.0

Control Our
Maternity Mêlée

A long list of schemers and ambitious domineers are zealously plotting strategies to monopolize our Maturity Wards. Ethnic, Nationality, religious, Intellectual, and women organizations are striving to inundate our populous with their particular humankind.

Example: Only African-Americans need run for office in Atlanta Georgia. And only Latinos need run for office in Los Angeles. Such dominations do not come about by happens stance. But they needn't be viewed as threatening or undesirable. After all, democracy is based on a government that represents the populous.

There are, however, birth rates for which we might be concerned (?)

The projected birth rate of homosexuals, for example, has been increasing significantly over the past decades—and promises to rise till it exceeds 50 %.

Currently, This proliferation is proceeding, unabated, for two reasons:

1) Homosexual census is not being taken— largely because there is no legal definition of sexual orientations, and
2) Religious authorities are preventing the public from knowing that our nation's majority is Bisexual, and the source of homosexuals.

Bisexual

Scientific studies by Dr. Alfred Kinsey and Masters and Johnson revealed that our genes control our sexual preferences and that they fall on a spectrum somewhere between Homosexual and Heterosexual.

Doctor Kinsey developed a scale from zero to six and defined the sexual preferences at each of the numbers. Number 3 is defined as bisexual and is referred to those who could have relationships with either same or opposite sex partners.

Based on *Natural Selection* the majority of our population falls in the center third of the scale.

Meaning: the majority of our citizens are bisexual.

Few bisexual realize they are bisexual. In fact most don't even know what is bisexual. Their motivations, inclinations, and behaviors are influenced by general social comportment.

Genetically, the majority of our newborns will be some where in the Bisexual range. Procreation, of course, is a mixture of two sets of chromosomes, and the resulting genes are not precisely predictable.

Chances are slim that any Bisexual off springs will ever be heterosexual.

And based on the growing trend, we can expect a goodly amount of our off springs will be on the homosexual side of the Bisexual spectrum.

Over the long run, the number of homosexuals will continue to increase. The fact that international Gay Olympics have been underway for few several years is a strong indicator of their Growing prominence.

If ever we hope to stop this trend, we'll have to make the majority of our folks aware of their Bisexuality, and offer them alternatives for procreating off springs.

Becoming aware

Determining one's sexual orientation is not a simple matter. Few people are ready or willing to accept the possibility they may be Bisexual.

But once they're determined to be Bisexual, and realize any of their children might be homosexual, they'd likely want to hear the details on alternative family creations.

The obstacle to determining people's sexual orientation is a belief, by certain religious sects, that sexual orientation is a choice that people make, and is alterable.

Many denominations, however, have acknowledged that homosexuality is determined by our genes and that gays have no choice of their orientation.

In spite of horrendous empirical data, many people still cling to their fallacious dogma.

Before we begin to hope religions will accept: that sexual orientation is determined by our genes, we've got to recognize the unchangeable manner in which mental fixations can prevent attitude changes.

We witnessed a classic case of this when the Jim Jones followers were willing to commit suicide, rather than forsake their beliefs. We need to realize: homosexual populous will eventually dominate our society.

Our growing homosexual population

It would be well for homophobias to understand why tens of thousands of GAYs take their lives every year. Rather than endure the persecution, abuse, and castigation.

From early youth, the gay child is recognized by other children as exhibiting feminist gestures and mannerism, and become a handy piñata-thwacking bag.

My secretary (we'll call her Peggy) told of how her son (we'll call him Jim) was coming home from school crying; horrified and mystified over the way the other children were teasing him.

Peggy sought psychological help, and tried to teach him masculine mannerisms—all to little avail. In his early teens, Jim attempted suicide.

Peggy enrolled him in a special rehabilitation at the Northridge Hospital. It seemed to help, and Jim was able to adjust, somewhat, to his intolerable condition.

A young man, at work, apparently found me a good listener, and ask me to lunch.

He was desperately searching for an answer to his homosexuality.

He bitterly hated his mother for what he thought was her domineering behavior that caused him to be gay.

I tried to convince him that his genes were the basis for his sexuality, not his mother's demeanor. His unbending orientation perpetuated his frustration, and he eventually committed suicide.

Two other men, from work, with whom I enjoyed friendships, committed suicide. Being a number six on Dr. Kinsey's sexual preference scale, I felt like the immune doctor with keen incite into the numerous gay's infliction; and knowing—beyond the shadow of a doubt—that sexual orientation is strictly gene determined.

I become bitterly incensed when pig-headed (and stupid) people doggedly claim that it's a matter of choice.

It took many years for the religious clergy to accept the fact that our earth circulated about the sun. And it appears the same longevity may be needed before it is agreed that: our genes determine sexual orientation.

24.0

Right vs. Left Brain

Why do we think and do as we do? And why do we become unshakably: Republican, Conservative, liberal, racist, homophobic, religious sect, nationally biased, etc.?

Believe it or not: Our genes make us what we are. All our mental traits—intelligence, emotions, attitudes, sexual inclinations, and personalities, and so on—are all determined by our genes—and are unalterable.

Then too: each of our two brain hemispheres treats our intellectual functions differently.

It's commonly agreed that our brain's left hemisphere enables the acquisition, storing, and recalling of vast amounts of information, and may also enable us to solve complex problems that have already been proven and documented, such as: scientific methods and procedures, medical ailments, and mathematical problems.

Doctor J. P. Guilford[1] concluded: *The most common compliant concerning college graduates as researchers is that while they do assigned tasks with a show of mastery of the techniques they have learned, they are much too helpless when called upon to solve problems where new paths are demanded.*

Our Defense Department once embarked on a massive program to develop "Artificial Intelligence."

It was an attempt to develop computer software that would allow the computer to actually duplicate the thinking process.

After millions of hour and billions of dollars, it was determined that no amount of software could ever duplicate the human thinking process.

Highly intelligent folks, such as: Doctors, Lawyers, Scientists, and professors, are dominantly Left-Brain—with minimal Right-Brain cognizance.

Their brains function much like large, high-speed computers.

And, like high-speed computers, they are unable to conjure up original thoughts and ideas, or solve hereto-unsolved problems; or accept original and undocumented ideas.

Doctors have boundless knowledge of hundreds of ailments, and thousands of medications, remedies,

---

[1] Guilford, J.P. "Creativity," American Psychologists, Sept. 1950

and cures, but being fully left brained are unable to diagnosis rare and previously undiagnosed ailments.

After 20 some years of research into the cause of the Muscular Dystrophy (MD) it was excitingly announced: The cause is due to lack of enzymes.

Five years later an apology was announced that the lack of enzymes was the **result** of MD. **Not** the cause.

Research Physicians, around the world, are searching for the cause of MD; convinced it is a **disease**.

There's a reason I suspect MD is NOT a disease. My son at age 6 was showing advanced signs of MD. His over-developed calf muscles were biopsied and revealed no sign whatsoever of MD.

I offered the following theory of Muscular Dystrophy to the MDA: (all to no avail)

My theory of MD

Our bodies are in state of tension throughout our waking hours, wearing down our skeletal muscles and not allowing them to rebuild (while in tension).

During deep sleep, our cerebellum releases all skeletal muscle tension—allowing them (muscles) to restore.

Fault: Cerebellums of the MD children do not completely release all tension and therefore do not allowing complete muscle restoration. Skeletal muscles of the MD children gradually lose strength, and eventually the lungs and vital organs fail.

Example of Left-Brain reticence

Not widely known, or considered, is the fact that dominant left-brains intellects do not accept unpublished thoughts and ideas.

This implies, for example, that left-brain intellects will **not** readily accept the validity or credibility of most of my right-brain solutions—offered herein.

Circa 1940, the entire medical profession disapproved, and vehemently condemned Sister Elizabeth Kenny for treating children with severe Polymyositis. After years of court trials and relentless condemnations, the medical profession eventually adopted her procedures.

Then to: Intellects of the first century were unable to believe the earth was circling the sun. And, currently, millions of antagonists are **unable** to believe our genes determine sexual orientation.

Right & Left Brain Distribution

Most people have some amounts of both left and right brain dominance. Their test scores in K-12 generally range from B's to C's, but also exhibit a semblance of creativity.

Left-brain students, on the other hand, generally receive straight A's; are recipients of scholarships, and show no signs of creativity.

Research studies years ago—searching for creativity in K-12 students—found D level student exhibited the highest levels of creativity, and found almost no creativity in the A level students.

An aside: students born with strong right-brain dominance will usually not have high levels of innate intelligence.

Our educational systems, being exclusively left brain structured, tend to consider right brain students *under achievers.*

Their assigned teachers are usually rated as sub-standard, and schools with a preponderance of right brain students are listed as failing schools.

Right-brain dominant People have several defining characteristics:

- Trend to day dream
- Tenacious Faults finders
- Intent on improving things
- Liberal thinking
- Solve unsolvable problems

Constantly seeking improvements (changes) defines a liberal ideology—the mainstay of the Democratic Party.

Our *Far, Far Better America* needs to recognize and fully understand something: Our brain hemispheres cause us to do favorable or unfavorable things.

Let us also recognize that our brain dominance is genetic, and unalterable. This means our ideology, creativity, intellect, amicability, impartiality, nangeability, and the like, are determined by our genes.

One criticism of the left-brain folks is their propensity to prevent new ideas or improvements from going forward—merely because they had never been implemented before, or because they represent a disruption of the status quo.

As John Locke said: *New opinions are always suspected and usually opposed without any reason but because they are not already common.*

Since left-brain dominance has difficulty accepting change to the status quo, this explains conservative ideology—the mainstay of the Republican Party.

25.0

Level
Playing Field

If History truly does repeat, then all my solutions, offered herein, are likely to be quashed, nixed, and forgotten. And our future will be *written on the Wall.*

Since the beginning of time, nation after nation has followed the same inevitability: intellectual elites seized the land, resources, most of the wealth, and the reining power.

A well-known axiom: *Power tends to corrupt; and absolute power corrupts absolutely.*[1] Every great revolution has erupted when the nation's masses were driven into desperation and destitute.

Power appears to be addictive and uncontrollable, for we see it growing ever so rapidly and seemingly without end. Intellects use their superior mentality

---

[1]   Letter to Bishop Mandell Creighton 1887

to amass huge fortunes and to acquire control of a nation's manufacturing facilities.

The Labor War

We might be inclined to condemn our hundreds of corporate giants for pilfering our industries and giving them to foreign nations (the primary source of our nation's income). But at least we should hear the real reason they did it.

For thirty some years our Corporations and Labor Unions have been entangled in a knock-em down drag-em out fight.

A law passed in 1937 gave the Labor Unions the right to organize, and added all sorts of protection.

Every year the Labor Unions added more and more fringe benefits, along with higher wages.

Corporations attempted numerous strategies to weaken the Union's—usually to no avail.

Circa 2002, all corporations proceeded to announce huge lay offs, like 20,000 to 40,000. They were merely bluffs.

Lay offs are very affective for striking fear into the union members, but the Labor leader saw this as a fear tactic and got the word to their members.

Finally, in desperation, the corporations shipped all our industries out of the country—leaving the Labor Unions high and dry.

The battle was over, and from all appearances the corporations won.

But, what of our nation?

Financial Ruin

With the source of our primary income gone, millions of people became unemployed; thousands of mortgages were foreclosed; consumer index fell; the stock market plummeted; airlines went bankrupt; car sales fell through the bottom; huge investment firms needed bail outs, and the list goes on.

Every conceivable reason for our recession has been bandied about, except the real reason.

Our depression—euphemistically referred to as a recession—is exasperating the chasm between or rich and our poor. The nationwide "Occupy movement" sparks a scary sign.

Usually such uprising are localized and spearheaded by a skilled organizer. But these uprisings are widespread and seemingly spontaneous.

While millions are living into destitute, hundreds of left-brain billionaires are becoming richer by the minute (?)

It would be so easy for us to condemn our billionaires of all sorts of devious skullduggery and underhanded shenanigans. But lest we go off half cocked, and leaping to conclusions, allow us to step back and see the big picture.

We could become philosophical, or religious and attempt to judge our billionaires while attempting to get some sort of retribution or appeasement.

If we believe there is a Hell, perhaps we might take satisfaction in reasoning that these people would be likely candidates?

According to Biblical text, a rich man has as much chance of entering Heaven as a camel going through the eye of a needle.

The only other place to enter would be Hell—according to the New Testament.

Rich people are rarely concerned about this, because: 1). They don't believe there is a hell, and 2) they don't believe there is a life after death. However. There definitely is a hell! It happens to be right here on earth.

Ebenezer Scrooge found this hell when the ghost of Christmas future took him into the tavern where his colleges were ridiculing and making fun of him (after his death).

We're all sensitively and vitally concerned about what people think and say of us.

History is replete with famous people that spent their waning years desperately attempting to mend their vile and greedy reputations—often becoming world-renowned philanthropists.

One tycoon—once touted as the richest man in the world—sent armed troops into the Pittsburgh steel mills to break up the labor unionizers. Nine men were killed.

This same tycoon spent his waning years, and over 400,000 dollars attempting to assuage his horrible image.

Thousands of statuses are erected all over the world to immortalize the memories of people who created outstanding pasts. This sort of thing is heavenly indeed—especially if the statues are still standing at the time of the immortalized death.

Hard to figure, but there must certainly be at least a twinge of guilt for those who amass obscene fortunes while billions of people are starving to death (?)

I suppose: along with their shrewdness to escalate holdings into massive fortunes there must also accompany a mental suit of armor that comforts tycoons till their waning years—hopefully with enough time left to erase a life time of reputation.

26.0

Our Copper Penny Scam

There's a reason 99 cents is tagged on to every retail price. It's a concept that dates back to the days magic elixir was peddled off the rear of horse-drawn wagons, touring the old west. And it confirms Barnum and Baily's axiom: A sucker is born every minute.

There are all sorts of tricks of the trade, but the most prevalent is the pricing of every product with the 99 cents attached to every price tag.

This 99-cent attachment has only one purpose. The dollar value of every item is reduced by one tenth of a cent to make the price more attractive. A product or commodity priced at $99.99 is more attractive than the same items for $100.00.

The US treasury calculated that by eliminating the penny as legal tender the US economy could save many billions of dollars. Retailers sent a host of high-price lobbyist to Congress and defeated the initiative.

A sucker every minute

Every consumer is considered a sucker when a product is offered.

Buyers do realize—at least sub-consciously—they are being scammed, but have no recourse.

And retailers . . . Who knows what they're thinking (?)

Apparently they're willing to manage complex bookkeeping and take the chance that consumers' might revolt.

The retail business community is composed entirely of left-brain personnel that have little or no perception of original thought processes. The possibility that the consumers might react favorably to the elimination of the penny is beyond these personnel's reasoning powers.

Eliminating the penny is a *change*. And any change is considered a threat to the Status Quo. And the Status Quo is a sacred cow; in essence, the coveted goose that lines the pockets of the giants.

The IRS seems to do just fine dealing strictly with dollars.

Penny Disposals

Once pennies are no longer legal tender, there will be billions of worthless pennies virtually everywhere. The metal is not used in any other monetary pieces, and wouldn't be of any use to our treasury.

People that possess thousands of pennies will hope to recoup some level of reimbursement (?)

Our banks would be the logical repositories, but should not be burdened with the count verification. And a counting machine should not be audible inside the banks. Weight scales could translate the weight of pennies into approximate dollar value.

The banks could reimburse owners and our USA Treasury could reimburse the banks.

27.0

What Are We
To Believe

We're becoming aware of the angry "Occupy" movement, although the underlying motivation isn't being well explained.

What's fairly obvious is the fact that one percent of our population owns and controls nearly all our government, and most of our economy.

For what it may be worth—stepping back and searching for the rhymes and reasons things like this happen—I'd like to offer some Food for Thought.

All living things have many things in common— such as survival. And survival brings with it the quest for as much of the necessities as one can acquire.

And it seems there are no limits on the amount of acquisitions, nor the means for acquiring such necessities.

It comes then as no surprise when we learn of tycoons acquiring more wealth than they or any of

.heir benefactors can ever use in their entire life times.

History reveals that the most intellectual individuals in every society have used their intellect to gain the upper hand in controlling the wealth and power of their particular settlements.

And in many cases these quests have gone on, entirely unabated, until the masses were subdued into bare subsistence—leading to revolutions and the annihilations of all the Intellects.

Although this cyclic phenomenon portrays innumerable historical records, with uncanny predictability, intellects the world over have seemed oblivious to the *"Hand writing on the wall."* A phenomenal fact comes to mind as we think back to the origin of mankind.

Unquenchable thirst for wealth and power has existed since the origin of mankind. Intellectual tribesmen given carté blanché for seeking the causes and cure of nature's tragedies and devastations welcomed the assignment.

With such enticing opportunities, the intellects undoubtedly sought privacy atop a high mountain, to concoct a conference with the *heavenly Spirits*. Predictably, the Spirits probably explained that the tragedies were reprimands for behaviors of certain tribesmen.

We can immediately see the tremendous power given to the intellects.

Entire kingdoms—although under the reign of kings have actually been controlled by intellects serving as religious clergy. Their power comes from inherent fear of the *Spirits*.

The *Spirits* undoubtedly asked the intellects to build fine edifices as magnificent meeting places in which to meet with the intellects. Foods and clothing worthy of the spirits became an absolute necessity.

Fear of the *powerful spirits* has served to amass huge hierarchies around the world and to strike fear into the populations.

As long as the masses believe conditions are as good as can be expected, and that and sort of improvements are hopeful at best: any improvements will remain in the care, generosity, and decisions of our intellects.

28.0

School Violence

Throughout the decades our schools have been devastated by hundreds of traumatizing school shootings. Instead of reducing the numbers, the rage continues on unabated.

Our teachers see first hand the underlying cause of this travesty. They witness the manner in which feminist mannerism of boy students are seen and tormented by senseless and misguided students.

As one of the Columbine trench coat Mafias put it: *Going to school is pure hell. Jocks push us into the lockers and throw stones when we ride our bikes from school.*

It's impossible to sense the horrifying pain and misery to which gays are subjected. Every year, tens of thousands are forced to take their own lives.

We become aware of the tragedies when the victims become so enraged they decide to take their tormentors with them.

Knowing full well the cause of school violence, the National Teacher's Association decided to teach students the truth of sexual orientation and the fact that it is strictly genetic.

During their annual convention, they were planning on adding the subject to their national curriculums. Religions from around the nation sent protestors to the convention and prevented the subject from being added to the curriculums.

This opposition happens to be terribly misguided, and stems from:

1) An explicit dissertation of sexual orientation might educate the masses to devastating results of submissively engaging in procreations—and a possible reduction in population growth. This overlooks the advantages of alternative nuclear family developments. (See 17.0 Save Our Newborn)

2) A fear that sexual orientation might be accepted, nationwide, as genetic, and NOT a choice. If this fact were to become nationally promulgated, one of the biblical scriptures might be open to question—placing doubts on the entire text.

This concern is grossly unfounded, since much of the Old Testament is to be taken at arms length.

And the New Testament does state that some gays are born so from their mother's womb (Matthew 19:12).

Religions stand at the gates of mercy and healing. But people born handicapped by their dreaded sexual orientation have nowhere to turn. Many beautiful examples of helping the handicapped are written in the scriptures. These wonderful examples are not just historic miracles, but are offered as examples for the believers to follow.

Three works of mercy come to mind:

1) The Church at large could make a resounding statement that: Sexual orientation is strictly genetic, and should be regarded the same as with any physical handicap.
2) Churches could set up gay classes
3) Churches could push for legalizing gay marriages, and could perform Gay weddings.

When the genetics of sexual orientation is taught in every public, private, and religious school, school violence will cease, gay suicides will diminish, gay persecution will be no more, and homophobia will be a thing of the past.

29.0

And,
In Conclusion

Achieving a Far, Far Better America is definitely no walk in the park. A huge slice of our nation is dedicated to preserving the status quo—another description for conservatives.

Status Quo made it possible for the upper class to strike it rich, and any alteration in these conditions threatens the goose that lays the golden eggs.

Clever intellect and shrewdness is what made it possible for a select few to gain control of our government and to amass huge fortunes.

Any alterations—though they may be highly beneficial (even to this select few) have the possibility of threatening the very conditions that made these obscene fortunes possible.

Care has been taken to present each of the offered solutions (herein) in ways to avoid disruption of status quo.

Naive as this may sound, there are, I believe, chances that a number of the *select few intellects* will feel this venture sounds like something in which they might care to participate.

Intellects being dominantly left brained won't readily grasp and accept many of the advantages of the above offered solutions. But just as some intellects eventually adopt emerging technological, they may, in time, incline toward acceptance and support of the Far, Far Better America.

It's hoped every citizen, from every walk of life, and every class level will catch sight of our *new* nation: unified, prosperous, friendly, and fair, with justice for all; and that this Far, Far Better America will catch the imagination of all Americans and will wet their appetites for the wonderful life yet to come.

These past 80 plus years have been, for me, a mixed bag of happening; lots of fantastic memories, lots of tragedies, lots of grave disappointments, and of course: exciting visions of great possibilities. Like Martin Luther King, I too have a dream. And like Moses, I can see the Promised Land.

Epilogue

America has plenty of room to grow. Over the past 200-plus years we've been laboring under self-imposed limitations, and subdued creative talents, producing the egregious conditions addressed herein.

We now stand at the threshold of real greatness and phenomenal world presence and have a remarkable opportunity to undo a second-rate existence. If our present generation fails to change our course, our nation's future is destined to continue down a slippery slope toward more and more dissolution of our industrial strength, and losses of our people's participation in our nation's destiny.

For our people to pursue a path to real greatness we've got to know where we're headed, and know the direction we should pursue.

Apathy—undoubtedly our nation's most serious weakness—stems from an absence of inspiring leadership, and from an election system that clearly disrespects voter's rights.

PART II

The thrust of this book, as previously noted, is to identify some of our nations most egregious weaknesses, and promote viable and feasible remedies. The objective, of course, is to provide our citizens with the best our nation can provide. But life is more than government and economic security. Our physical and mental health, can pose overriding concerns for ourselves, our loved one's and much of our society.

Medical Anomalies

The following theories are not claims of absolute certainty, but rather efforts to steer the thinking in directions believed heretofore not pursued.

Part II Content

Introduction 171
1.0   Muscular Dystrophy 173
2.0   Multiple Sclerosis 175
3.0   Overweight 177
4.0   Heart Failure 179
5.0   Strokes 181
6.0   Parkinson's 183
7.0   Alzheimer's 185
8.0   Apnea 187
9.0   Acne 189
10.0   Atrial Fibrillation 191
       About the Author 193

Introduction

I'm not about to throw down the gauntlet to the medical society. In essence, this treatise is merely to open a scope of reasoning aimed at exploring realms believed to be, heretofore, unexplored. Perhaps much has already been documented, and even opposed.

Each of these theories offers what I hope will be fertile food-for-thought. And none are intended as arguable or proven claims.

I'll be exceedingly grateful if any of these theories form a basis for original, and perhaps more valid findings.

In any event, I feel grateful for being able to bring-to-bear pressing concerns that have been uppermost in my thoughts for far too long.

Replies are most welcome and may be addressed to: fcoble@aol.com

1.0

Muscular Dystrophy

My son, at age 4, had difficulty climbing stairs. Biopsies of his overdeveloped calf muscles, reported: *No muscular dystrophy.*

Seven months later a Doctor in New Jersey diagnosed my son with Duchene's Muscular Dystrophy (MD).

The doctor explained what MD was, and how it develops. This was my first clew that MD was **not** a muscle disease.

Being an electrical engineer, familiar with electro-servo mechanisms, I asked the doctor if the cause might be an excessive neural feedback in to the muscle tissues. Unlike the typical doctor, he paused and thought for a while. Yes, he said, that sounds very plausible.

As my son's condition continued to worsen, I tried all the therapy recommendations provided by the Muscular Dystrophy Association, including have a swimming pool installed.

Massaging his calf and thigh muscles seemed to
prove his walking gat. Taking short walks seemed
ressive.

Studying medical text and journals to understand
e neural muscular control systems, I found
ur cerebellum performs the very same activity
erformed by an electro-servo mechanism, and, that
t releases all muscle tension during deep sleep.

Realizing that our skeletal muscles are in tension
throughout our waking hours—causing a progressive
deterioration—and that restoration cannot take place
while in tension. It reasons that restoration can only
take place during *deep sleep*—while all our skeletal
muscles are in paralysis.

If the cerebellum fails to make a *complete release*
during deep sleep, it would reason that restoration
would not be a totally complete.

After periods of hundreds of failed completions,
it would therefore reason that skeletal muscle tissues
would progressively deteriorate; thus telling us: that
a defective cerebellum could be the very cause of
Muscular Dystrophy.

To affect a possible cure, the MD patient might
be given augmented sleep inducements every night,
such as: sleep pills, tranquilizers, or some form of
anesthesia.

If the billions of dollars and tens of thousands of
research hours continue, in search for a MD *disease*,
the search could go on forever.

2.0

Multiple Sclerosis

Deterioration of Myelin covering the spinal chord causes short-circuiting of the nerve signals that control muscle movements.

This deterioration is similar to the melting of insulation covering electrical wires—resulting from excessive wattage.

Nerve signals that control Muscles movements are electrical in nature, and can generate excessive heat if the nerve signals increase their electrical wattage. Any numbers of malfunctions can cause excessive wattage, such as: increased nerve resistance, muscles demanding increased currents, or increased brain transmissions.

To determine the validity of this theory, extensive Electromyogram (EMG) testing could measure electrical signal strengths traveling through the nerve tissues of MS patients—keeping in mind that the cause is wattage, not necessarily electrical currents.

Recently, the affecting gene has been identified.

Yet no clear cause or remedy has been defined. This might allow for the consideration of the above theory (?)

Cures for MS might involve ways and means of reducing the wattage being generated in the nerve tissues. Vitamins with electrical properties, such as: selenium. Magnesium, iron, and zinc might be tried.

3.0

Overweight

Over weight people are being steered away from the one cure that could possibly save their lives and give them a new and most enjoyable life.

First lets agree on the cause of over weight. Nutrition is absorbed from our small intestines at a rate determined by our metabolism (genetic and unalterable), and when the absorbed nutrition exceeds our body's requirements, the surplus is stored in the form of *body fat*.

Less nutrition will be absorbed if we speed our digested food through our small intestines. And if the absorbed nutrition is less than our body's needs, stored nutrition will be extracted from our *body fat,* and we will lose weight.

Speeding digested food through our small intestines can be achieved in a number of ways. One way, is to eat half dozen bite-size prunes with fibrous cereal, and drink a glass of prune juice every day.

This may be supplemented with stool softeners such as Metamucil.

There are also many over the counter laxatives of various strengths that your doctor may recommend.

Note: When digested food is sped through small intestines (including diarrhea) the metabolism of over weight people will still absorb adequate nutrition to satisfy one's body needs. Plenty of drinking water might be needed if diarrhea occurs.

Note: Speeding digested food through the small intestines is not Anorexia—which happens to be rare mental disorder that usually affects people with normal body weight, that are unable to eat normal amounts of food.

Overweight people can safely speed digested foods through their small intestines without endangering starvation—as a result of their overactive metabolism.

It would be wise to talk to one's doctor, however, before starting an extensive laxative regime.

4.0

Heart Failure

Most frequent cause of heart failure is the lack of oxygen, resulting from: 1) obstructions in the arteries leading to the heart, 2) Inadequate inhalation, or 3) oxygen deficiencies in the blood stream.

There are a number of surgical measures to by-pass obstructions, but providing adequate oxygen should be our immediate concern.

To prevent build-up of plaque in the main arteries—a prescription drug called Plavic is being offered. This drug claims to prevent the collection of plaque on the artery walls, and is usually prescribed along with aspirins—a common anticoagulant

Aerobic exercises such as walking, jogging, bicycling, and swimming increase the rate of inhalation, and the rate of blood flow through the circulatory systems, thereby helping to flush clogging impediments from the walls of the cardiovascular system.

Aerobic means having or providing oxygen. Oxygen is probably the single most vital chemical elements in our bodies. Survival, growth, and functioning of every cell in our body are crucially dependent on oxygen.

Of course, this most definitely includes our heart and cardiovascular system. The devastating affect of arteriosclerosis of the arteries—calcification, loss of elasticity and hardening of the walls of the arteries—is one of the causes of high blood pressure, and oxygen starvation.

CAUTION:

Our heart can also be starved for oxygen in functional ways—as mentioned in a following chapter called Atrial fibrillation—and we should be aware and on guard.

If double vision, fainting or dizziness seem coming on, (a possible stroke) there is a procedure to follow:

Take a full aspirin (325 mg)
Inhale a full breath
Hold the breath for the count of ten
Release the breath
Repeat two or three times

5.0

Strokes

There are two types of strokes:

1) Cerebral aneurysm in which a blood vessel in a brain capillary balloons and ruptures or leads to the formation of a thrombi and or emboli that may block important blood vessels.
2) Lack of oxygen to the brain cells.

This thesis addresses only the second type of stroke. The key word here is: oxygen.

Attention is devoted to the various causes of blood restrictions, such as in the carotid arteries of the neck that supply blood to the head and neck. Attention is also frequently focused on cerebral blood clots resulting from plaques forming on the inner walls of cerebral vessels.

For avoidance concerns we need bare in mind that the damage to the brain is the *lack of oxygen*. For, should the supply of blood to the brain be adequate and yet lack oxygen, a stroke can occur.

Normally our blood carries adequate supplies of oxygen—especially during our waking hours.

But during deep sleep, our lungs tend to resign into a rest period in which the contribution of oxygen into our cardiovascular systems is markedly reduced. For the short period of time in which this reduction takes place the brain is normally able to subsist quit adequately.

A scheme in which: the deep sleep period lasts far beyond a safe range; systolic blood pressure level is far below safe levels—common during deep sleep—and; the brain's blood vessels are unusually restrictive, a massive stroke becomes imminent.

Regimens to clear the cerebral vessels, of course, are pertinent. Anti coagulants such as: aspirins can help to clear the blood vessel of plaque. For people with plague build up in the cerebral vessels, steps should be taken to maintain a relatively high systolic pressure to insure adequate blood pressure—to force the blood through the partial blockage—during the deep sleep periods.

When prolonged deep sleep periods are known or suspected, the patient should undergo a series of sleep disorder examinations, and possibly use oxygen every night.

6.0

Parkinson's

Experimental placing of fetal stem cells in brains of Parkinson patients has apparently had some successes.

My understanding is that the stem cells grow and are accepted into the brain mass. All of us hope and pray this procedure will gain wide spread acceptance and may some day cure nearly all Parkinson's patients.

My purpose here is to offer a theory of the basic cause of the Parkinson's disease, and in so doing conjecture a likely prevention regime.

As mentioned herein—concerning brain malfunction—I believe brain cell damage is caused by a lack of persistent and adequate oxygen supplies.

This lack of oxygen is not dramatic as in suffocation, but is rather believed to be periodic, and a barely perceptible deprivation. In fact, the oxygen shortage is likely to occur during extended deep sleep periods.

So it is during deep sleep that our lungs are made to produce adequate amounts of oxygen. When our bodies have adequate oxygen levels, our lungs actually go into a resting mode. And when our lungs have difficulty returning from this rest period, our brains send a shock wave to force return. This is known as Apnea (explained more fully below).

Most Apnea patients are not aware of their condition, and are not encouraged to seek sleep disorder analysis and therapy. Not too apparent is the fact that oxygen deficits, however small, will temporarily damages cells throughout our bodies—including brain cells. Nearly every cell has the ability to repair any slight damage. The brain, however, has an exceedingly slow capacity for damage repair. Note, for example the extreme difficulty the brain has for restoration following a massive stroke.

Parkinson's is therefore believed to be the slow, prolonged process of brain-cell damage, due to an almost daily oxygen starvation. Sleep disorder analysis should be performed any time a person suspects an Apnea type of condition. Oxygen generating machines might be set to go on during the early morning sleep periods—possible 4 to five hours into sleep.

7.0

Alzheimer's

Alzheimer's is believed to the slow, prolonged process of brain-cell damage, due to brief oxygen depravations that occur daily, during Deep Sleep. Sleep disorder analysis should be performed any time a person is suspected of an extended Apnea type of condition. And if tests show significant indications of prolonged Apnea, a person should take steps to minimize the damage caused by Deep Sleep prolongation. Oxygen generating machines might be set to go on during the early morning sleep periods—possible 4 to five hours into sleep.

8.0

Apnea

Already explained in the above chapters is the problem with acquiring adequate oxygen. Apnea is a rather familiar aliment that has been thoroughly diagnosed and treated. What seems to be omitted in available literature is any reference to the deep sleep involvement.

I believe Apnea anomaly occurs only during the period of deep sleep. The paralysis brought on by deep sleep lowers the lung functions to the point that our breathing becomes virtually nil. Increased duration in the deep sleep period can put our bodies into jeopardy of suffocation. The brain is constantly monitoring the body's oxygen status, and when it approaches a danger levels, the brain sends shock waves throughout, and the person suddenly awakes—gasping for breath.

As mentioned above, extended Apnea can stealthily cause brain cell damage and possibly Alzheimer's or Parkinson ailments.

9.0

Acne

While a teenager, my acne was so bad I was hospitalized several hours every week, over a three years period. They tried ultra violate ray, and an assortment of other treatments.

That was in the late thirties when little or nothing was really known about the causes of acne. For breakfast I was usually having cocoa, buttered toast, milk, and occasionally: pastries. Many years, after I was on my own, I was noticing that my acne varied quite significantly with my food choices, and that certain foods caused pronounced outbreaks.

I completely eliminated: butter, mayonnaise, regular milk, chocolate, fried foods, and pastries, from my diet. I resorted completely to skim milk (non fat). My acne disappeared. Occasionally, when eating out, I would order something containing mayonnaise, or perhaps regular milk, and pimples would erupt. Clearasil was very effective in drying the outbreaks.

Of course the problems tended to subside, as I grew older, but even into my 60's, I still experienced an occasional pimple. I often wanted to blame unusual mental stress.

After retirement, and relief from the strain of the job, I was able, from time to time; to indulge in one or more of the *forbidden fruits*.

As a health nut, I feel these forbidder foodstuffs are best avoided—totally unnecessary. And, of course, if stress and mental tension can also be avoided the physical benefits are quite rewarding.

Then too, we hear much about the benefits of fruits and vegetables, daily exercise, etc. Endurance exercises such as running, and swimming greatly help the complexion and body skin toning by supplying huge levels of oxygen to every cell in the body.

I believe that attributing facial bacteria to the cause of acne are, at best, a bit misleading.

10.0

Atrial Fibrillation

Atrial Fibrillation, according to Barron's *Medical guide, Dictionary of Medical terms, third edition*: "A condition characterized by rapid and random contraction of the atria of the heart causing irregular beats of the ventricles and resulting in decreased heart output."

I believe Atrial Fibrillation is a heart starving for oxygen. Why do I believe this?

It was a quit afternoon in the office, and one of my cohorts slumped over on the foyer sofa, clutching his chest. The Paramedics made it up to our forth floor in remarkably short time.

With the finesse of an orchestra director they had my friend lie stretched out on the sofa. One Medic used his stethoscope to listen for the heartbeat while the other contacted his hospital via radiotelephone. The listening Medic announced Atrial Fibrillation to the other and the hospital was notified.

The first Medic told my cohort to take a deep breath and hold it, under pressure. In an instant the fibrillation ceased.

Holding and forcing the breath forced increased oxygen into the cardiovascular blood stream, and got a goodly supply of oxygen into the heart muscles.

My cohort was advised that he could use this procedure whenever fibrillation occurred, but not to use it indiscriminately.

About the Author

(Found one day on my computer via "Picture clipping. PictClipping" with no sender identified)

One might surmise that an author of such visionary ideas and bold assertions might be imbued with strong political and world event opinions. Fatherless from age four, one of eight siblings, living through the great depression, a farm boy raised in Milton Hershey's famous Boy's School, a Marine in WWII, employed 43 years as technician/engineer with RCA, and residing in twelve different states, might account for his broadened, inquisitive and challenging curiosity. Daring to express coveted opinions may be risky at best and perhaps foolhardy at worst; since most people harbor strong opinions of their own—some in agreement with the author and others vehemently opposed.

Anonymous